SO TO SPEAK

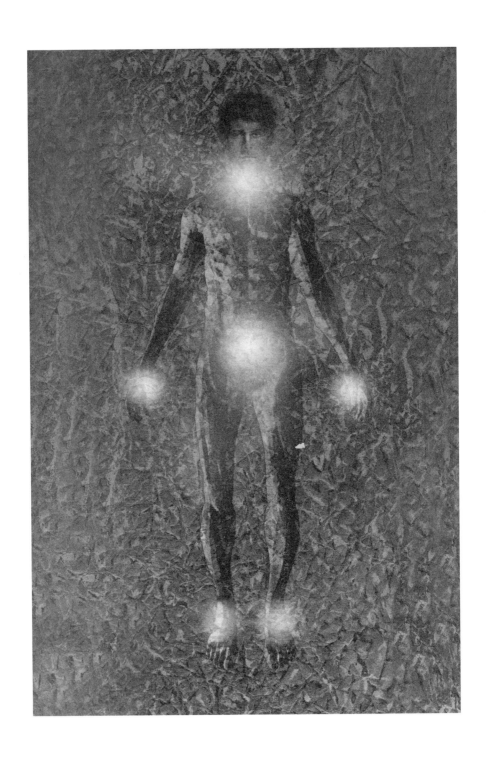

SO TO SPEAK

A Personal Approach to Voice

COLIN BERNHARDT

ILLUSTRATIONS BY
MILES LOWRY

Ekstasis Editions

National Library of Canada Cataloguing in Publication Data

Bernhardt, Colin.
  So to speak

  ISBN 1-896860-76-1

  1. Voice culture. 2. Acting. I. Title.
PN4162.B47 2001   808.5   C2001-910870-2

Acknowledgements:
Permission to use copyright material is gratefully acknowledged as follows: to Oxford University Press, NY for material from Virgil Anderson's *Training the Speaking Voice*; to Jonathan Miller for a quotation from his *The Body In Question*; to Vanessa Burnham for an excerpt from her unpublished translation of Ibsen's *A Doll's House*; and to Quite Specific Media Group for a quotation from Kristin Linklater's *Freeing The Natural Voice*.

Printed in Canada

THE CANADA COUNCIL | LE CONSEIL DES ARTS
FOR THE ARTS | DU CANADA
SINCE 1957 | DEPUIS 1957

BRITISH
COLUMBIA
ARTS COUNCIL
Supported by the Province of British Columbia

So To Speak: A Personal Approach to Voice has been published with the assistance of a grant from the Canada Council and the Cultural Services Branch of British Columbia.

Contents

Introduction

What is it that distinguishes people with great creative abilities like Glenn Gould, Charles Laughton, Maria Callas or Pablo Picasso? Why is it that 'ordinary' people are often content to stay 'ordinary', and don't take steps to change their ways of working and presenting themselves so that they become extra-ordinary?

One explanation may be that creativity emerges from a combination of IMAGINATION — vision, fantasy, ideas of what could be; and KNOWLEDGE — which involves how things are, how they were, how they function. Creation uses imagination and emotion to work on and transform the world THROUGH physical raw materials like paint and wood and stone or the human body, or even through non-physical but still earth-bound things like words and musical notes. Imagination is free and unbounded, but the business of how to transform materials on our planet requires knowledge, hard work and craft — in other words, TECHNIQUES.

These techniques must be acquired if we are going to be able to use them for creative activity and, because they involve practical skills and knowledge, they are in a sense straightforward to teach and to learn. Unfortunately, the process of acquiring techniques and knowledge can so easily become an end in itself. Teachers can easily grade us on them. The multiple-choice test is the extreme example of most modern education where, in Marshall McLuhan's words, "information is scarce but ordered and structured by fragmented, classified patterns, subjects, and schedules."[1] Knowledge, after all, is impersonal and claims to be 'objective', even though it often turns out later to reflect the biases and misconceptions of contemporary society, and to need adjusting.

Educational institutions, however, have a hard time with the imagination. When Albert Einstein said that imagination is "more important" than knowledge, he was drawing attention to exactly this problem.[2] Imagination is personal, subjective, unpredictable, and often alarming or confusing, like the world of dreams. How can the harassed teacher let loose this monster in the classroom? He/she usually doesn't — we simply go on studying for tests to test whether we have studied. Many of us in Western society seem to have become conditioned by these 'educational' experiences into mechanical ways of behaving — a kind of automatism in which our feelings and dreams are denied their part in the shaping of our lives.

There is a Malaysian tribe called the Senoi who have been reported as living in a society free of crime and mental illness, because they have learned to incorporate their dreams into their daily rituals. And communities in Bali treat every single member of their group as an artist: they all take a role in religious rituals, as dancer, sculptor, singer, doctor, weaver etc. The result, we are told, is a society with an amazingly high level of artistic achievement, as well as health and well-being.[3] I don't know how much utopian idealism there is in these reports ('noble savages' always sound suspicious), but whether they are true or not they make sense, because these peoples — unlike our own societies — seem to allow the expressing of imagination and fantasy to be an important activity in daily life. The artistic geniuses of our own society have clearly found a way, often by themselves and in opposition to teachers, to integrate their technique with powerful feeling and with deeply original imagination.

No one, for example, was able to teach the amazing Charles Laughton (famous for his role as 'Quasimodo' in the film *The Hunchback of Notre Dame*) how to stand, walk, sit or speak. His report card at R.A.D.A. in 1925 read:

> "Voice Production: He only attended a few classes.
> Careful work when he came.
> Acting: He is handicapped and knows it: he is too brilliant." [4]

In spite of Laughton's rustic looks and hunched posture, he believed so much in his own instincts that no one could question his style of performance: it was HIS. A friend described him as "a natural power, which he carried into all his projects . . . you felt about him that he wasn't only powerful, but a vehicle of power — something through which power passed, and was transmitted."5

The business of training people to become performers on the stage has always involved us in the attempt to combine imagination and feelings with technique, because performers have to be 'complete' people if they are to portray characters in all their completeness. But in training performers, as in everything else, a lot of practical knowledge and technique is involved, and once again there is a danger that techniques take over and become the main pre-occupation. This is especially true in performance areas which require exceptionally advanced technical proficiency such as dance and classical singing. But it is also true of acting training. Methods — including even the most famous Method, developed by Constantin Stanislavsky — become standardized and often idealized, as though acting is simply the development of a series of clever tricks involving the body, mind and psychology. "Be an ice-cream," orders Mr. Carp in *A Chorus Line*, and the poor student tries to 'feel' being an ice cream. Even the development of emotional openness and imaginative richness seem to be targets for a kind of routine methodology.

I had the good luck, first as a theatre student, then as a professional actor, to be exposed to a number of theatre artists who seem to have found some of the secrets of integrating 'technique' with feelings and imagination. In voice training, I was fortunate to work for a short time with Kristin Linklater and extensively with other teachers who had been trained by her. At Stratford I was introduced to mask work (and to many other acting skills besides) by the wonderful actor Powys Thomas (himself a pupil of Michel St. Denis). At Stratford I was also fortunate enough to have as a close friend the actress Helen Burns, who has given me more in conversation over the years than half a dozen professors of drama. Stratford, in fact, was a goldmine: I was privileged to work under the direction of a whole crowd of fine artists — people like Michael Langham, Jean Gascon, Michael Bawtree, David William, and Peter Gill.

So when I began teaching voice I did have an idea and a goal. But as my experience grew I found I wanted to spread out from this orthodox classical training where I had started, and to absorb ideas and knowledge and approaches from many other fields. Theatre, even though it is supposed to hold a mirror up to nature, often has a way of insulating itself from the real world, and falls behind what is happening. Since the 1960's, the growing acceptance of oriental philosophy, yoga, creative visualization, 'super-learning', spiritual quests, colour therapy, so-called 'inner ear listening', 'affirmation' and 'positive thinking' techniques; body-mind systems like those of Feldenkrais and Alexander; ritual and myth scholarship and healing processes like those of Jean Houston, and even some occult or mystical studies like shamanism, the Cabbala and a revived interest in the work of Rudolf Steiner, has led to a startling change in the way many people find meaning and direction in their lives — doing for them what the conventional religions used to do. Look at any bookstore and see the number of titles involving 'self-improvement'. This human potential movement is clearly a thriving business — which means, of course, that there are a lot of writers exploiting a hot commercial prospect, as well as many sincere people wishing to share their light with others.

As I began absorbing some of these new approaches in my personal life I found them creeping into my work in voice training. If actors in training are to find and release their emotions and their imaginative life, they need all the help they can get — and the classroom must be a place where their individuality is put first. They need to be encouraged in the feeling that the mystery and the wonder is here and now — here, in this room, at ten o'clock in the morning; that classwork is not some scientific preparation for a life that will be lived elsewhere, but an irretrievable moment of life itself, full of possibility for discovery and personal growth.

The work I have been engaged in has had gratifying responses, and some remarkable artists have described it as a turning point and a breakthrough in their creative lives. Much of the credit for this must go the teachers I have mentioned — especially Kristin Linklater and Jean Houston — and to countless books, articles and workshops, all of which I have cannibalized voraciously. But I have stuck to no one's dogma, and seem to break everyone's rules at one time or another. It just seems that my mixture of the orthodox and the intuitive, the straightforward and the crazy, the serious and the fun, has something to offer, and something that might be worth sharing.

Of course, anyone with a strong prejudice against soulless technique and methodology, can come up with their own solutions, which in the end, may come across as simply another methodology. R.A.D.A. voice teacher Iris Warren said of her work that it could not be written down, and her student Kristin Linklater was very aware of this when she decided to write her important and highly influential book. But no one who has worked with me has ever accused me of being too methodical!

I would like to thank Kristin Linklater and Jean Houston for their inspiration and personal guidance. I also extend special thanks to Michael Bawtree, who has helped so much in the preparation of this book, and whose advice and patience over the years has made all the difference. Bless you, Michael!

So here it is: a 'way in' to the mystery of vocal production which my students and I have had a lot of fun with, and have also found exhilarating and powerful. I hope the discipline of getting this process down on paper has not broken its spirit. If it sometimes seems not to make sense, then it is probably being faithful to my work: if on the other hand it makes too much sense then I may have gone badly wrong.

Before We Begin

So you are in the theatre, or you want to be — or you have simply come to the realization that your performance in real life could use a helping hand. You have picked up this book, looking for something. What will you find?

The book contains a series of ideas and exercises to help improve the natural qualities of your voice and release its power. It is an approach which attaches a lot of importance to your intuition and your sensory awareness. We shall be searching for the individual resources that lie within you as a 'unique person'. It is not a study of what is often called 'elocution', although we will be touching on formal as well as informal approaches to the voice. We shall be thinking of the voice as an outward manifestation of the power within you, revealing your own personal life force. When you speak, a unique person is heard, not simply a voice.

We shall be starting with physical and imaginative exercises which are designed to 're-condition' — or perhaps even 'de-condition' — your body, helping you to free yourself and find what is your true person. "To free the voice is to free the person, is also to free the mind and body"[6]. It takes daily practice, but the body/mind CAN become malleable, not only in its forms but in its functions. Since ancient times it has been known that images and words can alter the condition of one's own body — heart-rate, breathing pattern, perspiration systems, nervous state, mood, tear production etc. In our work we will be releasing images and words, to bring about bodily and vocal changes.

Let me say a few words about the release of energy. In these exercises you will, at times, be using large amounts of breath and it is possible that you may experience dizziness or feel faint, or even a mood-change. This is quite common. If it happens to you, don't be frightened: sometimes it signals a release of stress allowing a

So To Speak

fundamental change in your nervous system or your alignment. It often happens when people are about to make some significant discovery or are ready to overcome something which used to seem insurmountable. If and when it happens, try to cope with it positively: your habit of mind, resisting change, may try to prevent the new thing happening. Just remember that I told you this, so that if it happens you are not completely surprised. And don't give up on account of it. Dancers, singers and pianists go through many hours of what I call 'creative pain' before they reach a breakthrough. Why shouldn't this be the case for actors — or for all of us?

The making of images will be one of our chief tools in training. Our every breath, thought and action will be supported by image-making. Imagination — the making of images — is the key. In the words of a yogi, "Before words, there were images".

In our study we will be exploring, freely and joyously, an unconscious language of images and symbols. It is only by making them conscious that we discover them.

And now: let's go!

*Your entire head is now glowing with the Sun's force,
blazing with golden light...(p.23)*

I.

Posture

In order to reveal ourselves, or even the meaning of our words, we need to be free in the body. Our bones and muscles were formed even before we took our first breath — and ever since, our operating in the world has required us to hold ourselves up. From the first time we could stand, sit or walk, the spine has been doing its job.

The spine, it has to be said, is also one of the chief sources of pain and physical problems. Some tell us that this is because it was not 'meant' to carry the whole of the upper body — that we were designed as four-legged animals, and our getting away from the ground is the root of the difficulty. But spine problems also come from unnecessary tension, from habits of work and posture, and from emotional stress. It has been estimated that by the age of eighteen only 5% of the population are free from muscular and postural deficiencies, 15% have slight defects, and 65% have quite severe defects.[7] There is, therefore, a high probability that you, dear reader, have quite pronounced defects of which you may not be conscious.

It is the spine which connects our head to our torso, and since our whole bone and nerve structure depends on it, the spine is obviously of vital importance. There is really a sense in which it DEFINES our bodies — it is the physical manifestation of our bodily stance and stature in the world. Listen for a moment to the distinguished stage director Jonathan Miller, who is also a physician:

> Human action is a question of melody and harmony. Each muscle has its own melodic sequence. But the melody of each individual muscle has to be simultaneously harmonized with the tunes which are being played on all the others. The spinal

cord is the organ which integrates these two aspects of physiological function. The brain conducts and orchestrates them in the larger themes, composing them in the light of far-reaching considerations.[8]

Most people are not satisfied with their body. Often this is because society sets up images of physical perfection which the vast majority of us will never match up to. If you don't feel good about your body, your worries may well be making things worse. For an actor, the priority is not visual perfection but these three things: strength, balance and flexibility.

When you think about it, these are desirable not only for our body, but also for our mind and spirit. I believe that these attributes of mind and spirit can be developed as a result of becoming aware of the body and of how to use it. Through developing body awareness you can increase your mental alertness, your capacity to relax, your general health and your pleasure in life.

Let us now start by taking time to know our body better.

Stand upright in bare or stocking feet. Feel the weight of your body balanced evenly on your feet. Feel it not only in your heels and the balls of your feet, but also in the arch of the foot. The arch is an important place in which to find body energy.

Beware of putting too much weight on the toes. There are teachers who recommend putting weight here in order to present a forward-moving stance in the body — but the danger is imbalance, and it is balance which is all-important.

Sense the angle of the foot to your leg. Do the toes point outwards, or inwards? Are they in the position which best holds you steady, with weight in balance? Shift them a little, to find the most efficient position for them.

Imagine that energy is coming up from the ground and seeping into the arches of your feet. Imagine it slowly penetrating to the outer edges of both feet. You don't have to look down or do anything with your body. Just search for a sensation in your feet and register it — so that if you had to you could recall the feeling down there.

Concentrate on the feet now, one at a time. Feel the sensation your right foot makes as it comes into contact with the floor. Take your time. Feelings take time.

Now do the same with the left foot. Be aware of its sense of touch, and of its weight-pressure. Feel the space between the toes, and think whether it affects the weight-placement of your body. Is there a space in the arch and under your toes? Yes: feel it. Imagine that this space is storing the energy from the ground and transmitting it to the whole foot.

The foot is a work of art. As you stand there, think of it as a completeness: think of its structure and architecture.

Now move your awareness up to your ankles. Take time to receive messages from the surface of the ankles, and from the ankle joint within. Let them be for a moment the whole focus of your concentration.

Sense now your two legs and visualize as much as you can about them. Feel the energy in them drawing up from the feet, from the ground. Become aware of the space behind your knees. Is there tightness there?

Feel your thighs, right into your two hip-sockets. Start letting the energy rise into the whole lower part of your torso. Take awareness into the genital and anal muscles. Make some tiny movements in the anal muscles to bring them into your awareness. (Try not to be embarrassed by making yourself aware of these areas: they are important for getting into contact with deeper breath. Since they are an area which can cause slight embarrassment, we will refer to them as 'power stations' or 'the power area'.)

Now, with awareness stationed in the power area, feel the pelvic and buttock muscles. Sense their shape and make tiny movements so that you can feel their connection with the lower spine. Can you feel anything in this tailbone area? Try. Now go on moving your awareness up the entire spine, to the middle (thoracic) area, and then on up to the place between the shoulderblades. Continue into the neck, through the (cervical) vertebrae which take the spine up the nape of the neck and into the skull.

Don't be concerned to DO anything physical: just 'work' with your sensory awareness. Is your consciousness of the various parts of your body having any effect on it? Do you get any sense of floating or freeing? Watch for it — it may happen. Sometimes I see people doing this simple, happy exercise, and beginning almost at once to stand a little taller and with more grace.

Has anything happened to your breathing? We haven't thought about it for a while — see if it has changed its pattern.

Now let your searchlight of awareness move into the bony areas of the skull. Sense the eye-sockets and imagine going right through the brain to the back of the skull. Can you sense any tension around here?

Now recall and sense the slow journey through your body, from head to toes, that you have just completed. The sensations you have felt add up to the complete YOU. We have toured the country. We will be back.

Find a chair and stand with the back of your legs lightly touching the front edge of the seat. Place your feet fairly wide apart, with the toes pointing slightly outward — if this is comfortable for you. Let the head and neck fall gently towards the chest, by their own weight. Let the knees bend in line over the toes, and reach with the hands towards the floor, while at the same time sitting. Do not raise the head. Pause, and take a few easy breaths.

Now, slowly raise up the upper part of the body and sit with arms hanging at your sides, allowing the chest to be lifted and the head to float upwards, as though floating on top of the spine.

Allow yourself to enjoy the deeper breathing that has been stimulated. Avoid putting the chin down, and pause for a few moments.

Now, let the head and neck fall toward the chest by their own weight, letting the chest bend downward too, so that the back curves. Pause again, breathing easily.

Without changing the relationship between head, neck, and back, bend forward, reaching towards the floor with the hands between the feet. Pause again.

Align the knees over the feet with toes pointing slightly outward. Then, still without changing the relationship between head, neck, and back, rise a little way from the chair by pushing the feet equally against the floor.

Now, fully stand by straightening the knees, allowing the chest to fill and to lift, and the head to float upward and to balance itself once again on top of the spine.

Walk around the room for a minute or two, to allow any changes in the body to continue. Be aware of any changes that may have taken place.

Place yourself with your back against the wall. Now take one pace forward, bend your knees and drop back against the wall, making sure that the small of your back is in contact with the flat surface.

Once the position is established press the whole upper back, neck, and head against the flat of the wall.

Then, from the bent knee position, push away from the wall with one brisk movement, and start walking in this aligned position. Register any change to your normal stance and walk.

Now let us link up actual physical movement with movements which take place in the imagination. This is the first of many times that we will be working to explore and strengthen this vital link.

Stand comfortably, with knees relaxed and eyes closed. Focus on your breathing for a moment, as a way of directing your attention inward. Make sure you are balanced on your feet as in the first exercise. Sense your contact with the ground. Scan your body for possible tension — especially check the neck and shoulders.

Now raise your right arm and stretch it slowly upward, sensing the shifting alignment of the muscles all over your body as you do this. Feel the stretch in your fingers and your hand, your arm and shoulder, and your torso.

Now, with equal awareness, lower your arm. Repeat this several times, always with the right arm.

And now go through the same process, still with your right arm, except that this time you raise it only in your imagination – imagining as vividly as possible all the same physical sensations which you experienced before.

Now stretch your 'real' arm, up and down, and now once again your 'imaginary' arm. Alternate several times.

Repeat the process with your left arm, first 'real' and then 'imaginary'. Now alternate between 'real' right arm and 'imaginary' left arm, and then vice versa.

Rest. Notice any changes in how you are now standing. People with regular tension in the neck and shoulders often experience great release. You can invent further exercises on this model, for other parts of your body.

Finally, let us complete these introductory exercises with one that takes the imagination several stages further. Is it to do with posture? Judge for yourself — not by what it says, but by how you feel and carry yourself when it is over.

Lie down and close your eyes. And allow your body to 'become' the images that I describe.

Imagine that above you is the Sun. As you know, without the Sun there would be no life on our planet. Its energy in the form of light and warmth gives life to everything it touches.

Now feel this energy entering your body. Imagine it penetrating every part of you. Now imagine your spine as a tunnel, and that all the Sun's energy, its golden rays, are concentrated there, flowing up the spine-tunnel. Feel its incredible power rising through your spinal column. It is powerful, so powerful that it cannot be contained. It starts to thrust out of your spine and into the small of the back. It finds its way into your rib-cage, around your sides and into the chest. Take time to feel this life-force within you.

Now let it grow into the shoulderblades and down into your arms: biceps, elbows, lower arms, hands, fingers. Feel the Sun's rays in your hands and streaming from your fingertips.

Keeping your sense of the Sun's life-force, let it overflow out of the spine into your neck, penetrating your ears, the back of your head, and up to your forehead. Your entire head is now glowing with the Sun's force, blazing with golden light. Feel it through the sinus passages behind the eye-brows and cheek-bones, and moving deep into the nasal chamber, cheeks, jaw, mouth. Feel it touching your tongue, roof of mouth, palate, throat. Feel the energy flow down through the open throat, down through the chest, all the way down to where you breathe –in the centre of your body, just below your navel. Let it flood through your vital organs: liver, spleen, kidneys, intestines. And now you are

Posture   23

saturated with the Power of the Sun. Enjoy it. Take your time. Feel it tingling in every pore of your skin.

And now, feel the Sun stretch out from you into the room, every inch of the room. Feel it flooding out from the room into the rest of the building, growing out into the town, the countryside, the whole country, the continent, the planet. Expand with the Sun's Power, as it moves out to the planets, to the whole solar system. Go right out with it as it joins other Suns, travelling into the universe, and then into another, and another, and another. See how far you can go towards infinity.

When you are finally there, feel the ONENESS of the life-force; and that you have lost your form... you have... become...the Sun...

["......mmm...zzzzz..."

Hey, guys, just a minute – don't go to sleep! This process needs you to be fully aware.]

Caringly, gently now, start coming back with your power. Back through the universes and planets, back to our earth, and back to your place – your body: the temple. Feel the power coming back through your toes, balls of your feet, arch, heel, top of your head, neck, fingers, hands, thighs, power area, chest, all the way back to your chest, and down to your centre. Imagine that all the power you touched upon way out there at the ends of the universe is contained now in one tiny dot behind your navel. Know this. It's yours. Rest within it.

Finally, memorize the sense of oneness that you have experienced, and rise slowly to your feet, re-creating that same sense in an upright position. Do it slowly, because you might be dizzy. Walk around. Register how you are, how you feel. Look at others around you, if you have done this in a group. Share the oneness with them.

So To Speak

This isn't the moment for analysis of what you have just done. Is it a posture exercise? Students' reactions in the past include:

"I lost myself;"

"I didn't think I was breathing."

"I could feel the breath as though my body breathes."

"I felt nauseous – but it was worth it."

"For the first time ever, I seem to be in touch with my body."

Let us leave this first set of exercises with this thought:

"We first create an image of what we want the body to do or become. Through repeated efforts, the body begins to do it. Your body becomes your partner, and begins to want to work with you. Body parts and muscles are not just lumps of mindless bone and tissue. They have reactions and memories, limitations and potential. The body has its own wisdom."[9]

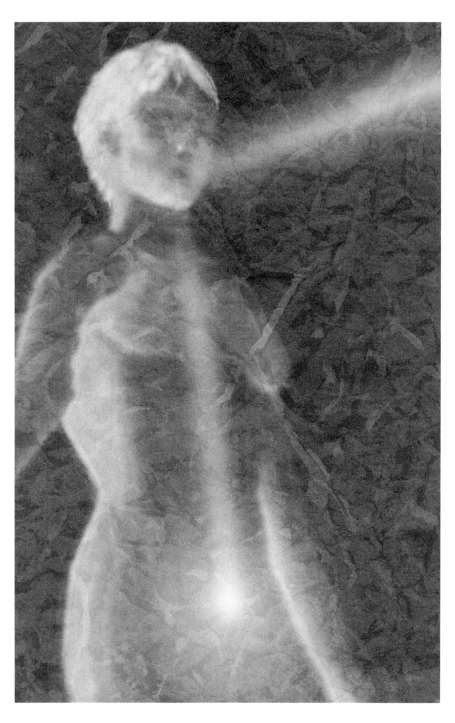

Sense the power deep within you that drives the breath... (p.31)

II.

Breath

Wisdom and Spirit of the Universe!
Thou Soul that art the Eternity of thought!
And giv'st to forms and images a breath
And everlasting motion!

William Wordsworth[10]

We are all familiar with the fact that, a few seconds after we emerge from the womb, we are given a slap which surprises us into taking the first breath. From then on, year after year until our last moment, we draw in air and release it again every few seconds, without conscious effort, drenching our blood with the oxygen that keeps us alive.

All other animals and birds do the same thing. Most of them have also developed ways of using the release of air to make noises with: cows moo, elephants trumpet, birds twitter, dogs bark. And we humans do all sorts of things: we cry, scream, laugh, grunt, whistle, hum, sing — and, of course, we speak.

Most of the noises that we (and animals) make, come from vibrations set up in the larynx by the breathstream as it passes through on its way out via the mouth and/or nose. The noises that animals and birds make are for the most part genetically programmed. Many species have developed a wide range of sounds, and use them to communicate mating calls, alarm signals, territorial claims, and in some cases well-being, frustration or pain. Humans also make genetically inherited sounds: we do not have to teach a baby to cry. But humans have developed this simple communication system infinitely further than any other creature, and have an immeasurably wider range of communicating sounds under their control. We normally start learning to speak around the age of two, and learn without trying. By the age of six, most of us are reasonably able to communicate in our mother tongue.

Because the breathing and speaking processes (in normal situations) happen without much conscious effort, and because both are so reactive to our social and emotional environment, the way we breathe and the way we communicate through speech often retains characteristics of our childhood learning process — and sometimes scars from emotional situations that have affected our breath pattern, pitch and tone of voice. Many of us become accustomed to functioning with only a small percentage of our voice potential.

I personally believe that everyone can benefit from voice work to extend their communicative power: the voice is the person. But for an actor such extension is vitally necessary. To accomplish it we have to bring the process of speech out of the habitual, semi-automatic world where it usually resides. Later, in our chapter on diction, we will be looking at the whole question of speech habits. But let us start by exploring that first energy source without which speech cannot exist — the breath.

Immediately we encounter a paradox which will continue to concern us as we progress through this book. Many of the body's processes can be described as though the body is a machine. The body IS in a sense a machine, an input-output construct — drawing in energy and transforming it into activity or product. The more we know how the body works, the easier it is to think of ourselves as inhabiting a complicated mechanism. But machines are man-made, and are programmed and predictable, within the limits of their efficiency; whereas the great glory of human beings is that we have consciousness and will. And it is our will, our spirit, that gives point and direction to the strange bag of bones which is our body. So it is possible when thinking about 'breath' to liken it to a bellows with a rubber hose coming out of it, or to go into an exact study of the complex mechanisms of breathing. But if we do this, we are in danger of becoming not conscious but SELF-CONSCIOUS about breath, like an anxious factory worker tending a temperamental engine which seems to be taking over.

The following exercises, then, are just a few of the many which I use, and are designed to help us become conscious of the breath with-

So To Speak

out too much science. Anyone who wishes to study the fascinating mechanics of breathing and voice can do so in any reputable book on the subject. Let us start here instead with a thought from George Leonard's *The Silent Pulse*:

> "At the heart of each of us, whatever our imperfections, there exists a silent pulse of perfect rhythm, a complex wave of forms and resonances, which is absolutely individual and unique, and yet which connects us to everything in the universe. The act of getting in touch with this pulse can transform our personal experience and in some way alter the world around us."[11]

Remember the exercise with which we began our work on posture? In our mind's eye we travelled through our body, becoming sensorily aware of each part of it in turn, from the toes to the top of the head. Later, in the Sun exercise, we received the Sun's power into our body, feeling that power grow and spread until it filled the universe, then returning to compress its energy into our centre.

These travels through the body are one of the ways of making it our own, becoming comfortable with it as our home and our partner. So we shall be doing a lot of it — becoming seasoned travellers! — and each time finding something more on which to build our sense of the Self as a completeness, a unity.

Let us begin this work on our breath with another exploration, but this time taking with us a new idea:

Lie down, palms of the hands facing up, and once again start at your feet, becoming aware of how they are placed in this prone position. This time, talk to them directly, asking them to relax in every part. Tell them they are becoming heavier, heavier. Then become your feet and answer softly, or in a whisper, "Yes, we are relaxed. We feel heavier and heavier. . ." Continue with the dialogue, gently and conversationally, talking to the various parts of your body as to close friends or to sisters and brothers. ALWAYS ANSWER BACK FOR THEM. This is hard to do at first, and the idea makes people giggle. But you will be surprised how soon you can 'think yourself into' the different areas of your body. When you reach the scalp let your voice take on a sleepy, dreamy quality, as though the voice itself is beginning to do what it has been telling the rest of the body to do: relax more and more deeply. Continue the dialogue with the forehead, eyes, cheeks, lips, chin and jaw, the voice becoming ever more relaxed, like sleep-talk — until, when it reaches the jaw, it can barely function and the body-parts can do little more than murmur a reply.

We have 'found' a voice for each part of the body. Voices need breath. And so we have found breath not only in our lungs but in all our body. The body breathes. Feel the breath. Everywhere.

Imagine now that you are on an ocean, and that the waves are moving you up and down. Up. . . and down. . . Up. . . and down. . . Your whole body is moving on the waves. Go with the rhythm.

Where is the source of the ocean, of the waves? Focus on your lower belly. Feel it move out as the breath draws in, and back in as the breath recedes.

Now focus on that centre, where the sun's power was crammed into a tiny dot. You have found the source. Sense the power deep within you that drives the breath. . . the place where you must go to draw on all you wish to hear, utter, or create. Hold your focus for a minute or two.

And now, with your concentration still on that centre of your being, open your eyes and very slowly roll over, and get up on to your feet. Your breath will come a little faster as you make these movements: feel it coming always from that centre of power. And now slowly start to walk. Walk around, turn, walk in different directions, always slowly, always feeling the motor power coming from your centre.

If you are doing this exercise with others, stop now and look one of them in the eyes. Look at them from your centre — as though the power to see comes from the power centre, up through your body and out through your eyes.

In the Middle Ages they talked of eyebeams, and how the eyebeams of lovers twined together when they looked each other in the eyes. They also talked of eyes as "the mirror of the soul." Look in your partner's eyes, and see through the eyes to their centre, as they see through your eyes to your centre. Centre to centre. Experience this for a few seconds.

Then move to another partner, and to another. Don't miss anyone.

And now move slowly into a circle, keeping the mood of quiet concentration. Not everyone will be there at the same time: there is no hurry. When you have taken up your position, remember again the feeling of being lulled by the waves of your breath. Recreate this image and start breathing in time to the movement of the waves — up, down, up, down. As you breathe, allow your body to sway gently with the waves. As more and more join the circle, the waves become one ocean — powered now by all your centres.

Now, finally, begin to make a sound on the beat of the wave. Make it a two-syllable sound ending in an "M" sound — but NOT a real word: "dee-nam", "ray-om", "sah-vem" — anything you like. The sound can be semi-chanted, and you will find it natural to make the sound in time with every one else. And remember, it is rising from that same power centre which drives the waves of your breath.

When the sound is established, let it slowly fade off the breath, still letting the breath move and sway you. . . and slowly, slowly, the ocean is silent. And calm.

In the silence, listen to your breath. Listen to the sounds still resonating. In your own time, when you are ready, break from the circle, and rest.

The importance and value of an exploration like this is perhaps self-evident. No vocal development can take place without the very strongest sense of rooting breath — and therefore sound — in its source at the centre of your being. Finding and 'stocking' this centre is not a scientific procedure but an imaginative adventure.

At the conservatory I was taught to be aware of three phases of breathing:

1. Thoracic or Chest Breathing, in which expansion and contraction of the lungs takes place in the upper part of the torso.

2. Medial or Central Breathing, in which most of the expansion and contraction takes place in the lower rib area.

3. Abdominal breathing, in which breathing takes place mostly in the waistline area.

These divisions of breath-type are clearly scientifically arrived at from studying various ways in which people breathe. In order to understand the divisions you must experiment with them yourself, and begin putting breath into the various compartments of your upper body as a way of understanding what is going on. You will also be told that central breathing is generally the most effective of the three, and so you will begin to think about breathing in this central area.

Central? Haven't we just been talking about the centre as the place where breath comes from? Let us leave these physiological categories on one side for the moment, and work another way.

For hundreds of years, people have known of the power of colour, and its associations with our emotions. Colours have their own vibrational wave patterns, and their own temperature. And some studies in Russia have suggested that certain people can even sense colour by touch. Let us now make use of some of the qualities of colour, exploring the ways in which it can serve us as we go deeper into developing our breathing/feeling centre.

Phase One

Lie down on the mat, on your back, and let go any tension you may feel. Close your eyes. Breathe easily, and remind yourself of the source of the breath.

Now, imagine that the air of your breath is coloured, that it is a red vapour. Draw it into your body, and imagine it going down, down, deep into your power stations. 'Feel' the energy of the red colour suffusing this whole area and absorbing any tensions that may be there. Then, as you exhale, imagine the red breath drawing the tensions from the area and releasing them from your body.

As you breathe in the red air again, imagine it this time expanding to fill those same areas again, but now, free of tensions, so powerful is it that its energy begins to overflow, radiating around the outside of your pelvic area, like a magnetic field: so that when you exhale, the red energy remains, and when you breathe in again, the red energy accumulates in those power areas, becoming part of the driving force of your breath-stream.

Lie still for a minute or two, sensing the power of your new-found 'red energy.' Now, without losing that power, imagine that the new air you are breathing in is orange. Breathe it in, in your imagination, all the way down from your hips through your calves, knees, shins, feet, toes. And as before with the red, feel the orange suffusing all these parts of the body. Can you sense a difference between the quality of orange and the quality of red? Yogis assert that red is 'energy', and orange is 'enthusiasm'. Does this make sense for you? Try to feel it.

Now, as you breathe, imagine the breath infusing both these areas — red in the power stations, orange in the lower limbs. Breathe it in fully for a few minutes. This completes the first phase of colour breathing.

Rest.

Phase Two

You are now ready for the second phase. I will list the progression of colours, and you will need to absorb each in the same way as already described — take all the time you need:

Imagine that you are breathing in the colour gold, and that it is filling the upper abdominal area, through to the small of the back. Gold is associated by Yogis with 'wisdom.'

Now breathe in the colour green, and feel it suffusing your heart, filling your chest up to your collar bone and back to your shoulderblades, and spreading into your arms and hands. Yogis associate green with the quality of 'love.' This completes the second phase of colour breathing. Rest.

Phase Three

Now breathe in the colour blue, and feel it entering your neck, your face up to the eyebrows, and the back of your head. Blue is associated with 'knowledge.'

Now breathe in the colour purple, but imagine that instead of breathing through your nose or mouth, you are breathing in the colour purple through your forehead, at the spot between the eyebrows where the pineal gland is located, and which mystics sometimes refer to as 'the third eye.' (You are of course not actually achieving this, but you will not find it difficult to imagine it.) Let the purple spread through your brain. Purple is associated with 'the spiritual.'

And now, finally, breathe the colour of white into the top of the head — imagining if you can that you are breathing it in THROUGH the top of the skull.

The colour white represents all the colours combined, and is therefore associated by Yogis with the divine. It arrives into our consciousness now to complete and unify the spectrum. Let it do this by imagining it first drowning the purple, then the blue, then the green, then the gold, then the red, then the orange, falling down, through, round and over your body in a radiant shower of white.

This completes the third phase of colour breathing, the three phases together constituting the entire breathing cycle.

Continue breathing now with a sense of all the colours, and the unifying white, and sense the stimulus of these layers of feeling/colour through your body. It is difficult not to complete this exercise without a uniquely powerful and pervasive supply of breath energy, linked with the thoughts and feelings associated with each of the colours.

Rest. Notice how you are breathing without effort. The breath breathes you.

Lie down on the mat, with your hands at your sides. Become aware of your breathing from the centre, and follow it in, out, in, out. Take eight or ten minutes for this.

Now focus on your heart muscle in the middle of your chest, and see if you can detect its beat. It has a pulse, like 'pa-pom, pa-pom' — an iambic beat (weak/strong, weak/strong). Don't be surprised or worried to sense it. It is there like a tide going in and out. If you cannot actually sense it, imagine that you can — most great discoveries start in the imagination!

Focus on the gentle beat of the heart in the middle of your chest, and feel the energy of that muscle as it creates that weak/strong rhythm. Enjoy it. Let the energy driving the heart muscle overflow into the small of your back for three or four minutes.

Now take the energy and sense it flowing into your thighs . . . your knees. . .the arches of your feet. . . the palms of your hands. . . the solar plexus. . . the back of your head — always sensing that this is 'feeling' energy, provided by your heart muscle.

After you have touched on all these parts individually, see if you can expand your senses to feel them all pulsing at the same time. Let it grow till it is a single pulsating, throbbing sensation. ("I AM the pulse," said a student.)

And now, in this state, notice your breathing. It is effortless. No more energy is needed than what you are now detecting, for all your breath-vocal needs.

Take this energy which is now in your breath, and allow it to arrive on your lower lip, by lightly making the sound "fffff". Feel the connection between the breath in your centre and the breath on your lip. Don't work at it. You don't need to do any more than the energy of your exhalation makes happen. The energy, in other words, is effortless.

Enjoy it: enjoy sensing the stream of breath as it arrives from your centre, easily, casually — registering the point where it begins, in your centre, and the point where it arrives — on your lower lip.

Now, with the same awareness, gently touch on a scrap of sound — Hey, be careful now! Just because we mentioned sound, there's no need to huff and puff and start getting prepared! It is exactly the same thing as you have already been doing with your breath — effortless action....

Say 'aaahhhh'. What is the difference between 'aaaahhh' and 'fffff'? One of them has a little vibration — observe where the 'aaaahhhh' begins — and where it arrives on your lips.

Put the palm of your right hand on the middle of your stomach, and notice what is happening to your centre, as you make the sound of 'aaaahhh' once again... and again. The vibration begins here, and the sound is linked to a physical movement — in fact it IS a physical movement.

Now, leaving your right hand on your stomach, raise your left hand and hold it a few inches away from your lips, with the palm facing you. Make the sound of 'aaahhh' again, and this time notice how the energy of your breath, which begins under your right hand, can be felt arriving on the palm of your left hand as the breath stream emerges from your lips. As you repeat the sound, hold your hand further and further away, working to continue hitting the hand with the energy of your breath. When you have stretched your arm to its fullest extent, continue projecting your breath stream past it and into the room. In this way you will sense both the source of the breath and its effect on the space around you.

Relax your hands, and continue with some more "aaahhhs". Then try the same sound but with your mouth closed — bring your lips together. Notice that this changes the sound to "mmmmmmm". Repeat "mmmmmm" several times, searching for where its vibration is coming from.

Take a rest. We will come back to this in a minute.

Now, I want you to give a genuine sigh of relief. Perhaps you are glad it didn't rain today, or happy that this exercise is beginning to make sense — anything as long as it is something you feel genuinely glad about. Sigh, and as you sigh be aware of where it is coming from: feel the movement in your centre — just where you have placed your hand. A thought, a feeling, a breath, a movement, a sound — all finding their source in your centre.

This, believe it or not, is the most important action we will be concerned with in all our training. The sigh you have made is your very own: it springs from your own feeling and nature. It will be the key to putting your personal stamp on all your utterance.

Since we have gone this far, let us go a little further. Let us, in a sequence of steps, gradually build up a sound that will serve as a 'conditioner' for all the sound we make: a kind of 'archetype' of sound, containing the basis of all sound within it.

1. Let us start by repeating "aaahhh," and then change it gradually to a two-syllable sound, each syllable beginning with an 'h' sound: "ha-haaah." The first syllable is short, the second elongated: "ha-haaaah". Make the sound several times.

2. Now make the same sound, "ha-haaaa," on the outbreath of your 'genuine sigh of relief'. Remember, this requires 'effortless energy'. Do it several times.

3. And now, repeat it but this time close your mouth by gently bringing the lips together, and enjoy the "mmmm" vibration which forms on your lips. Repeat several times, always focusing on the sensation of

vibration on the lips.

4. Repeat the sound once more, but this time, at the very end of the "mmmm" sound, open your lips again, to let the tail-end of the sound flow freely forward.

And there you have it — the archetypal sound. On paper it looks something like this: "ha-ha-mmmmmmmmm-mah."

Let us sum up the action and value of the complete sound:

• The sigh-of-relief impulse which initiates the "ha-ha" is generated in your centre — you cannot create it any other way.

• The sound resonates through your upper body as it travels to the lips for "mmmmmmm" — which in turn causes the bony chambers of your skull to vibrate.

• The release of the "mmmm"sound on "mah" sends the message of the sound outward and forward, making everything that comes before it a kind of preparation.

• The sound is then complete.

Summary

In all our work from now on, we shall make extended use of this sound. You will take time to absorb its full potential and effect. Understand that it encapsulates much more than just a sequence of sounds. In a strange way it harnesses and directs the power of your breath, linking inside with outside, inaudible with audible, feeling with expression. It is a sound which must become as comfortable, and as much a friend to you, as an old shoe. You will be amazed to know the actors and actresses of every age and temperament, who will be found sitting in their dressing-rooms before the show, and making contact one last time with the source of their energy, through the wonderful sound of "ha-ha-mmmmm-mah."

You will notice that we have completed three exercises without so much as a mention of the diaphragm — the powerful muscle situated at the bottom of the rib-cage which pulls down to inflate the lungs, and releases to deflate them. For anyone who wishes to explore the physiological details, books are readily available. But it is my belief that the group of exercises introduced here establish a feeling/sensing basis of breath without which all the physiological knowledge in the world will be of little use. Make your own choices. But be sure that you understand the reasons why these exercises are so important.

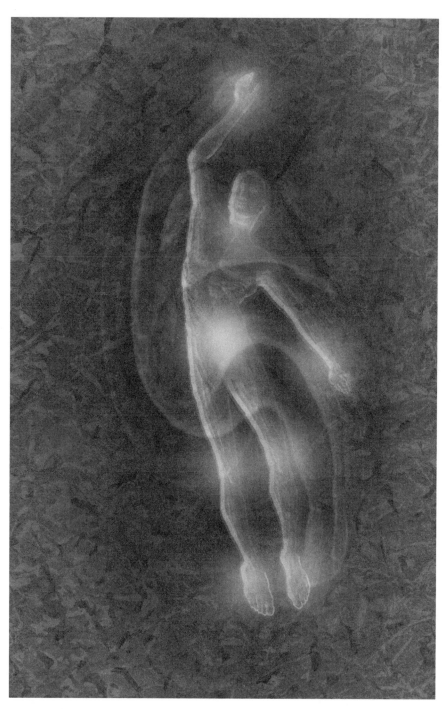

All of a sudden we are caught up in a vortex, a whirlpool... (p.60)

III.
Relaxation

Since early times mankind has recognized that the process of thinking and feeling produces actual physical changes in the body. We blush from embarrassment, we can be speechless from excitement, cry from sadness or from joy, and tremble from fear. A physiologist puts it more scientifically:

> All emotions are accompanied by physiological changes: fear, by palpitation of the heart; anger, by increased heart activity, elevation of blood pressure and changes in carbohydrate metabolism; despair by a deep inspiration and expiration called sighing. All these physiological phenomena are under the influence of nervous impulses, carried to the expressive muscles of the face, and to the adrenal glands and to the vascular system in rage.[12]

These external 'signs' — and the unconscious body language that goes with them — will often tell other people what is going on inside us. Once again, it is instructive to consider what happens in our early life. When we are babies we exhibit these signs naturally. We are hungry, so we cry — we don't plan it: it just happens. But within a year or so of being born we are already beginning to realize, "Aha! When I cry, Mother always comes. So when I want her, I shall start crying." The crying becomes a communication device — even though it may still produce all the same physiological effects as a 'natural' cry. What started out as an instinctive response becomes a way of influencing people. And so acting is born: we imitate nature in order to affect others.

An understanding of this relationship between the workings of the mind and feelings and the way they show themselves visually, is essential to the performer. Great actors are able to let us see 'inside' a character, revealing the character's feelings not only through the things they actually say, but also by their use of breath, tone and pitch of voice — and by the way they walk, and turn, and move their hands, and hold their heads. Some theories of acting concentrate on getting the performer to think and feel at all times exactly the way the character must be thinking and feeling, in the conviction that if this is done honestly and sincerely then the body language, vocal tone and pitch etc. will all automatically reveal what is truly going on inside. The opposite of that approach would be to get the actor to learn a whole list of gestures, signs, movements, ways of speaking etc., and so to be able to select the gestures needed to convey to the audience what the character is thinking and feeling from one moment to the next. The problem with the latter approach is that the audience may easily sense the phoniness of the acting: the gestures and movements can look as though they are 'stuck on.' The problem with the 'natural' approach is that our feelings and thoughts do not all show themselves clearly in our bodies: some of us learn early in life, in fact, to hide what is really going on inside. What most experienced performers do involves a mixture of the two — moving from the inside outwards, and from the outside inwards.

Unfortunately it is not only the character's thoughts and feelings that we show to the audience: we can also — without wanting to — show signs of how we feel in ourselves. Fear of embarrassment, fear of failure or of forgetting, fear at the very thought that we are being watched, can all get badly in the way, leading to symptoms like trembling knees and hands, hurried breathing, dry mouth, rapid heart rate, diminished vocal power, perspiration, nervous giggling, and so on. And when we try to block these negative thoughts and stop our lips trembling, hands quivering and knees shaking, we of course tighten up the muscles of our face and jaw, of our arms and legs and neck and hands.

Even performers as great as Sarah Bernhardt and Sir Laurence Olivier have admitted to experiencing fear before a performance. In fact 'stage fright' is perfectly normal, often hitting us before any big effort we make — before exams, or an important match, a business deal or a major speech. The body responds to the fear by releasing adrenalin into the blood stream, and this often gives us the courage and the stimulus necessary for a good performance. But if the fear leads to tension, it can paralyze us so much that we cannot function. "Relaxing of the muscles should become a normal phenomenon ... only then will it cease to interfere when we are doing creative work."[13]

The stage performer has a further challenge in the problem of tension, because of the need to re-create the emotional states of the character being played. If these emotional states are re-created effectively they can themselves increase the chances of the performer being paralyzed by tension — tension produced by the feelings of the character. The effect can be the same — limbs become rigid and the voice tight, hoarse, muffled.

We have already confronted the need for relaxation in our chapters on posture and breath, but it is of such central importance to the development of the performer that it calls for a chapter to itself. I would like to deal with it in three stages:

1. The root cause of tension: the need for self-belief.
2. Ways to relaxation and the discovery of the emotional centre.
3. Image-making.

Stage One: The Root Cause of Tension — The Need for Self-Belief

My work in training the performer suggests that tensions are often a surface cover-up for something deeper within the person, and that the dynamic of relaxation is tied up with knowing one's own self and believing in oneself. Freud thought that such tensions are necessary because they set up a basic anxiety against which one must place defenses in order to keep healthy or survive. This may be the case, but if the performer is so tense as to be paralyzed, he/she has to find a way to release tension in order to function. It is interesting to note how few performers today realize the inhibitory effect caused by lack of self-belief. The Greeks considered the body as a temple for the soul. It was Plato who said that "the healthy soul has power within itself to make the physical condition as perfect as it can be."[14] And Stanislavsky wrote:

It seems that if you lay an infant or a cat on some sand to rest or to sleep, and then carefully lift him up, you will find the imprint of his whole body on the soft surface. But if you make the very same experiment with a person of our nervous generation, all you will find on the sand are the marks of his shoulderblades and rump — whereas all the rest of his body, thanks to chronic muscle tension, will never touch the sand at all.[15]

Because of high anxiety in our present time, our conditioning in society often makes us so self-critical that we close off much of our personal power and freedom. Inner pressure then results, as tension builds from the denial of our feelings. I once had as a student a young woman of breathtaking beauty with considerable talent and vocal potential. This performer, placed in a performance before a live audience, would lose all physical grace and vocal power. It was a surprise, because during class and rehearsal time a vital performance had seemed to be in the making. Obviously something was wrong. Our sensitive and personal approach to training took time, but after a lot of exploration the demon eventually revealed itself: the performer was plagued by a negative inner voice that kept uttering thoughts of self-hatred.

One day, working on a particular performance piece, I told her to use her own sense of natural physical beauty to reinforce the character's portrayal. She stopped everything, truly amazed by what I had said. She exclaimed that surely I was joking, or my taste in beauty was in question: astonishingly she had never for a moment thought that she was beautiful. The first of many releases followed, revealing inner self-hate, sense of unworthiness, lack of confidence in her intelligence and interest for others, and overall a profound sense of inadequacy caused by unnecessary doubts and fears. During performance these inner feelings would well up and become a devastating block. No wonder the quality of performance went awry, when her inner self was so loaded with negative tension.

I have mentioned this one incident because it is a problem for many of us: no matter how cleverly and secretly we disguise it — that demon inner voice always putting us down. If the soul does live in the body, imagine its confusion! The importance of our own self-belief is

So To Speak

more often than not the gauge by which to measure the quality of our performance. As performers we cannot remain ignorant of our inner negative judgements. The Buddhist philosopher Chogyam Trungpa Rinpoche said:

> Negative emotions are like manure. If you recycle them and work with them they become like a compost heap, they nurture growth. If you don't deal with them, but just push them aside, or ignore them, they are nothing but a pile of shit.[16]

It would be wrong to claim that negative feelings about ourselves can always be put right with a mere exercise or two. Sometimes their cause lie deep in our childhood experience, or in a sense of guilt about things we may or may not be right to feel guilty about — or they may even come about as a result of a chemistry change caused by an allergic diet. But there is no harm in trying out the following exercise, which, corny as it may seem, has helped a lot of people.

By the way, do you need this? Well, ask yourself, "How do I look to myself right at this moment?" "Wonderful," you may say — in which case you may skip the whole thing if you like! But it is amazing to find so many 'wonderful' people, and especially actors, who think they are ugly, unworthy and inadequate. Through the exercise you may even get in touch with unexpected ways in which you are not loving yourself. Try it and see.

'Affirmation' is based on the well-tried idea that negative inner voices can be countered with other inner voices — ones which we supply consciously ourselves. Have you ever attempted to conquer self-distrust through positive affirmation — forcing yourself to accept the idea of belief and positive qualities in your own person? It sounds simple, but it can bring results. After all, if you don't say these things about yourself, why would you expect anyone else to say them? Here we go then:

Lie down in our usual comfortable position, and — remembering our colour-breathing exercise in Chapter Two — start with two or three minutes of breathing your favourite colour. When you are fully at peace and in tune with your colour, begin the 'ha-ha-mmmmmmmm-mah' — the archetypal sound that we have already discovered and practised. Feel for the vibrations, and imagine them breaking down the tensions in your body. Pause, and be silent.

And now, in this calm and peaceful state, affirm to yourself:
> I am beautiful and can be loved
> I am kind and loving, and I have an important gift
> I am talented, intelligent and creative
> I am happy and am doing good work
> I am in love with the world and am a vital part of it.

Speak directly to yourself, and imagine (image-make) that your love and goodness is beaming out to the world.

Say to yourself, to your life-spirit:
> "I love you. You are wonderful, beautiful and sensitive."

Be silent. And now affirm:

> I am open to receive the energy of the ever-abundant universe.
> The more I receive the more I give. All good flows through me.

Imagine yourself in a supremely happy situation and create the image of someone coming up to you and telling you wonderful things about yourself. Slowly people start entering one by one and agreeing with these wonderful things about you and telling you how wonderful you are. Imagine seeing the respect and love in their eyes.

Now create the image of yourself on stage, with people cheering you on with love and appreciation for your work. Hear their cheers and applause. Let it ring in your ears. Go to centre stage and take a moment for recognition and thanks.

You are a unique person. You are the pure energy that flows through the universe. You are no longer starved of vital feeling. You begin to accept your goodness and share it with others. If you look around you will see you are loved.

Be silent. And now affirm:

> I am loved and accept it
> I accept myself completely as I am
> I like myself and that is what counts
> I express myself freely, fully, and at ease.

Affirm:

> I am free and healthy.
> I love and accept my body.
> I am good to my body and my body is good to me.
> I am energetic, full of the life-force.
> My body is balanced in perfect harmony with the universe.

Create the image of yourself for a few moments in this 'ideal form', as a perfect being surrounded with healing light.....

Stay still as long as you like .... and then slowly get up and sense the world around you again.

As you get up you may well feel an immediate effect on your confidence and sense of specialness. If you suffer from a poor self-image you can find yourself reacting like a starving child being nurtured with loving sustenance. Get into the habit of repeating the exercise regularly, tailor-making the things you affirm to your specific needs. Through affirmation you can rebuild your self-image from what you are to what you want to be.

Stage Two: Ways of Relaxation & Importance of the Emotional Centre

Our work of 'affirmation,' as a way of establishing trust and confidence in ourselves, leads naturally on to this section, in which we will explore some of the most commonly used exercises for the release of unnecessary tension.

UNNECESSARY tension? Yes. It's important to remind ourselves that although unnecessary muscular tension has to be avoided, we cannot dispense with tension altogether: otherwise we would be simply blobs on the floor, like jelly-fish. Most of the muscles attached to our skeletal frame are in fact arranged in an intricate system of pulleys — for every action that we make in using one set of muscles, another set of muscles must be relaxed. When we lift something in our hand, for example, the muscles that we use for pushing our hand down are relaxed, allowing the muscles that pull up to do their work. You can see at once that if both sets of muscles tense at the same time, the arm would be rigid and paralyzed — and this is what happens when we get a bad attack of nerves or stage-fright. So one of the first things we need to master is economy of effort — in order not to interfere with the muscles that are doing the work.

We should remind ourselves yet again of one other thing: to work from the centre. By centering our energy, as we found in Chapter Two, we discover the source of power. The diaphragm and all the muscles in the act of breathing become part of a supportive musculature that connect with the dynamics of speech and action. It is vital, then, to remember that all things originate from the centre: every gesture, sound and breath. Relaxation allows the power to communicate freely and naturally.

Let us then work with two exercises for relaxation, and then with a third which offers another way of finding and drawing upon our centre as the source of power.

Lie on the floor, feeling your oneness with it, and 'letting go' with every part of you. We are pulled towards the earth by gravity — don't resist.

Now, sit up straight. What muscles did your brain give instructions to tense? Which ones do you need in order to keep this position? Be very specific — make sure that you are only tensing the muscles you need, and that the others around them are as relaxed as they were when you were on the floor.... And now lie back, and relax fully again.

Now stand up. What muscles do you need to tense to keep standing? Think slowly through your body to identify the ones which keep you from giving in to gravity. Make sure, once again, that those are the only muscles which are working. Experiment by relaxing for a few seconds each of the muscles which you find to be firm and holding..... Lie down again, and relax.

Now take up a kneeling position. What muscles are working now? Are they different from before? Are new ones coming into play? Are your shoulder muscles as relaxed as before, or have they started to pull your shoulders up? Make a conscious effort to release any parts of you which seem to be tense without doing a specific job..... Relax on the floor again.

Where do each of these movements come from? A neurologist will tell us that the brain is sending instructions to the muscles. But this way of thinking turns the body into a mindless robot, carrying out a master's wishes. So think of each movement as something which springs from your 'centre', which we started to find in Chapter Two. That way, your body and mind act as one.

Now — working from your centre again — get up, and sit in a chair. Once again, observe your body carefully. What muscles do we need in order to sit? Are your arms and hands relaxed? Are your shoulders as free as before?.... Relax. Rest.

Through this exercise we begin to see the difference between 'working' muscles, and muscles which are tense without doing any actual useful work. This kind of approach is sometimes referred to as an 'isolation exercise' — we isolate the muscles that we need.

In the next exercise we apply these principles to the muscles of the face. The face is a part of your body particularly prone to unnecessary tension, and of course, this is more visible to an audience than almost any other kind of tension. This exercise helps us become conscious of what our faces are doing, and helps us develop the same economy of effort that we worked on in Exercise One. It is another 'isolation exercise'.

Stand or sit in front of a mirror.

Raise your eyebrows sharply as though in surprise... and then lower them sharply in a frown. Repeat for two or three minutes, and pause. Make sure that only the muscles of the eyebrows are moving, and that the rest of your face is not involved. Check in the mirror.

Now flutter your eyelashes as fast as you can — imagining a strobe light if you like. Do it for a minute if you can, and then pause. Once again, and for the rest of the exercise, check that you are only working the muscles you need.

Now rotate your eyes, so that they look in every direction. Don't let them be lazy – make sure they make as much movement as possible, and that they really observe as they turn. Do this eight times in one direction, and then reverse for another eight rotations. Pause.

Now turn your eye-gaze in to the centre of your nose — so that you are looking cross-eyed. Repeat this eight times, and pause.

Wrinkle up your nose, as though you are smelling something awful.... and release. Repeat several times, and pause.

Now make a slow grimacing smile, stretching the closed mouth as wide sideways as possible, so that the cheek-bones lift. Repeat several times, and pause.

Bring the lips together and forward, like a tiny knot — as though kissing a baby. Holding the forward position of the lips, open and close them several times. Pause...and rest.

These two exercises are specifically devoted to muscular relaxation. But as we have already seen, relaxation is at the heart of all our work, and we have already been employing relaxation techniques as part of our explorations in posture and breathing. As we continue you will find that we come back again and again to the need for our body to be free of any tension which might block its expressive power.

Let us end the section with another approach to centering — one that takes us back to a time when we were centred without conscious effort.

Imagine yourself as a tiny baby — don't be embarrassed. As a performer you must be prepared to play many roles. Try and find the playful innocence and uncontrolled freedom that a tiny baby experiences.

Start by lying on the floor and imagining yourself as a baby in a crib or playpen. Start moving your arms and legs as a baby does. Now start playing with sounds, feeling the pleasure of making sounds with your voice, lips and tongue — as though discovering them for the first time. Forget the habits of sound-making that you have accustomed yourself to, and let yourself feel free, and even silly — if you are feeling silly then you will be doing it right. You will also be relaxed enough to discover the place in your body which you want access to for creative energy.

Start with: "ma-ma-ma-ma-ma"...
and then continue in sequence with:

"da-da-da-da-da....
la-la-la-la-la.....
oo-oo-oo-oo-oo....
koo-koo-koo-koo-koo.....
goo-goo-goo-goo-goo......
dee-dee-dee-dee-dee...
die-die-die-die-die...
da-doo da-doo da-doo da-doo..."

Now, with very loose lips, say:

"bhu-bhu-bhu-bhu..."

And now continue with your own playful sounds.

Notice how the making of these sounds feels physically, and where the feeling is in your body. Be aware of the vibrations as though they are something you are discovering, as you freely and aimlessly say "muh-muh-muh-muh". Do it with a bubbling sensation and keep it going for a while, as though it were a delicate thread of sound you are spinning out of your mouth, like a snail's trail.

Vary the pitch and the length of the sounds. With cheeks puffing say:

"puh-puh-puh-puh-puh".

Now do the same sound but sustain it:

"puuuuuuuuh, puuuuuuuh, puuuuuuuuuh".

And now allow yourself to see where in your body the energy for these sounds is coming from: not from your throat but from the mid-section of your anatomy.

Finally, explore the same 'baby' approach to making sound, but using a text, piece of poetry or nursery rhyme. Place it in your centre before you say it. Take time to feel it there, and speak it first in the same way as the way in which you made the baby sounds. Then slowly enunciate it with more and more clarity and power, but be sure to keep the sound coming from the same central base. You will be surprised at how it rings!

Stage Three: Image-Making

We have been working conscientiously through exercises in breathing, posture and relaxation, and have begun to build up self-confidence through affirmation. I like to think that we are now in a state of relaxed alertness in mind and body. If Linklater is right, that "to free the voice is to free the person, is also to free the mind and body," the reverse is also true: freeing the mind and body is part of the process involved in freeing the voice. The 'person' in fact is all these things together: mind, body and voice. The free voice sounds from out of a whole person.[18]

So now, before we move on in the next chapter to the most voice-specific part of our work, let us do what we often do when we need a change — take a journey. But this is no idle vacation. I want for a short while to open the door to an area which is fundamental for the actor: the process of imagining, of image-making.

Stanislavsky wrote that "Every movement you make on the stage, every word you speak, is the result of the right life of your imagination"[19]. In all acting training methods, time has to be spent helping students develop the ability to visualize what is not actually there, to imagine the details of a character's surroundings and life and inner feelings. Out of that imaginative work come the decisions about how to present — how to BE — the character on stage. And since the voice is part of the character, the voice is also included in the total person that we become.

We have already used our image-making ability to help us explore our bodies, and have taken advantage of the way in which image-making can actually affect us and change us. We began with the 'Sun' exercise, in which we imagined the power of the sun radiating through and upon us. We moved on to colours, linking them to our breath. And we have just been using the same process to affirm our confidence in ourselves. All this prepares what we might call a healthy 'environment' for our voice. But as performers we must always face the fact that though we are spending time and effort to make our voice our own, that same voice of ours must also become the voice of the characters we play. This looks like a contradiction: but this is where image-making can also help us. The journeys we go on here can help us to construct the image of a bridge, a pathway, between ourselves and the characters we play. Without being able to imagine that bridge — and to cross it — we remain where we are, locked within ourselves and so not free at all.

Incidentally, what has this to do with relaxation? More than you might think. William Bates, the American ophthalmologist who wrote his controversial *Better Eyesight Without Glasses* as long ago as 1918, developed a 'natural' system for image-building based on the fact that seeing involves both a sense impression gathered by the eye and the interpretation of that impression by the brain. He believed that "when you can remember or imagine a thing as well with your eyes open as you can with your eyes closed your vision will improve promptly." When something is imagined sharply and clearly, the eye relaxes, attains its normal shape and sends impressions which the brain recognises as sharper. "Perfect memory of any object INCREASES MENTAL RELAXATION..."[20] So, if Bates was right, the capacity to visualize accurately and specifically seems actually to help our minds relax!

Here we go then: two journeys out of ourselves...

Journey One:

Sit on the floor comfortably, knees raised with arms resting upon them, and eyes closed. If you are alone you must read the following passage, and then imagine the journey — or imagine your own version of it. If you are in a group, one of you can speak for the rest. It must be taken slowly, with time for each event to have its moment.

"Let us imagine that we are each of us in a boat, alone, voyaging out into the calm ocean. Then all of a sudden we are caught up in a vortex, a whirlpool. We feel the boat taking us spiralling down to the bottom of the ocean. There is a door. On the door is a sign, maybe of a lion, or a sea-serpent. As we see the sign, the door opens, and we step into a long corridor, leading down a vast tunnel..."

So one image-making journey begins, using a simple narrative to draw us into an imaginative experience. The journey involves us in a transformation and a disorientation — from air to water, from calm to storm, from a straight line to a spiral. Once we have reached the bottom, the tunnel can lead us wherever we want, to whatever we need to achieve the specific goals that we as performers have marked out for ourselves. It may be that it leads to Othello's room and we find ourselves there with Desdemona coping with Othello's jealousy. Or perhaps we reach the world of Llaregyb, under Dylan Thomas' *Milk Wood*, and find ourselves clattering down the streets of the little Welsh village. The point is that through imaginative journeying we can transfer ourselves in a full and powerful way into worlds normally closed and strange to us. The imagination so vital to the performer begins to soar. Out of it he or she makes a new dramatic reality.

Journey Two:

Let us voyage again. An actress is to play Lady Anne in Shakespeare's *Richard III*. She is relaxed. She imagines a colour to breathe with.

Then: imagine your colour becoming a ray, a light beam that rainbows out away from you. Walk out on that light beam, journeying away from the present, from today, from this place. Walk on that beam back through the centuries to Chaucerian England and encounter Lady Anne, meeting her for the first time 'on location' — her home, her palace. Study her intensely. How different is she from you? Her clothes — what colour does she wear? Her hair style, colour of skin, posture, height. Listen to her breathe, the 'sound' of her voice...

Go closer. Sense her perfume, her energy. Where does it come from? Where is her centre? Where is yours?

Now come back to your own life and remember what it felt like to get dressed this morning. Recall the sensations of putting on your blouse, your skirt, or whatever. Now use the same sensations to 'put on' Lady Anne. In other words, slip right inside her form. Feel what it is like to go inside her feet, her hands, her breasts. Does she fit? How will you make adjustments, so that she or you will fit? Then walk with her. You can even hear her thoughts...

So another bridge-building begins, another pathway between you and a strange experience which you must make familiar to you.....

Journeying: Conclusion

I have found that these journeys, which can take anywhere from ten to thirty minutes, lift a group of students out of themselves and have the power to inspire and excite, as an actual journey might. They are also a wonderful way of beginning work on a specific dramatic text. We so badly need the capacity to move out of ourselves, and to imagine new realities. Once the idea is clear, we have a wonderful free ticket to every kind of place and time and character and experience.

Invent new ways of building bridges, and make this kind of journeying a regular part of your learning.

Summary

Our main concern in this chapter has been to explore ways of attaining relaxation in body and mind, through both psychological and physical work. We have shown that this is a necessary prelude to everything we do on the stage. But it is, of course, vital for healthy and expressive use of the voice.

Equally vital, as we have seen, is the need to project the voice from the centre. We must remember, after all, that the vocal cords are simply another set of muscles doing their job through appropriate tension: the particular muscles that stretch the vocal cords need to be in a state of balance just like the other complementary sets of muscles that we discussed earlier. If muscles groups work against each other, if there is unnecessary tension in the cords themselves, then they can be strained. In everyday conversation you are unlikely to put great strain on the larynx and, even if there is tension, at close range and for brief periods of time no strain will be detected. But when we are required to project the voice over to an audience in a large space, and if — to make matters worse — it is not projected from the centre but only from the larynx, there can be serious vocal damage, resulting in permanent breathiness, hoarseness and unevenness or loss of tone.

The vocal cords play their part in the total rhythmic pulse of our bodies. So do the articulating muscles which we use to shape the sounds we make, and which we will be exploring in the next chapter. As we shall see again and again, it is only by working from our centre that we develop harmony in the body, and therefore in the sound-making mechanism. By drawing everything — breath, thought, sound and even necessary tension — from the centre, and sustained by the imagination, our body becomes an 'environment' for our speaking. Good speech in other words is carried out with the whole being. The voice flies from our body into the air in all directions with ease, shape and sounding clarity.

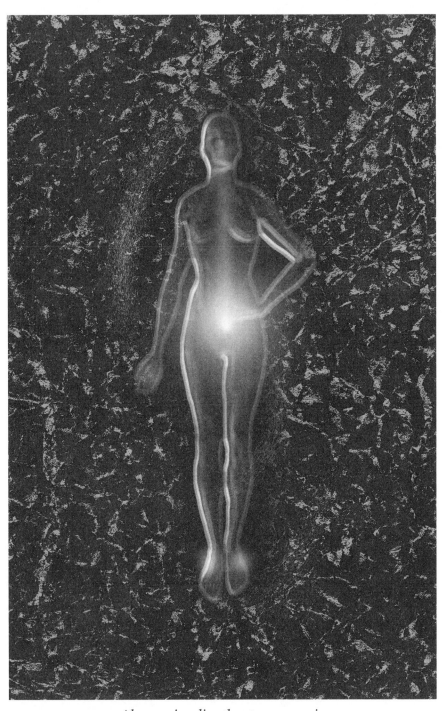

*Always visualize the stream coming
from the source, the centre of your body... (p.85)*

IV.

Articulation

Our work up to now has concentrated on the preparation of the body for effective speech. We are now ready to deal specifically with the use of the speech organs and their function in articulation.

Articulation is one of the most bewildering of subjects for the actor in training. In the first place it gets so easily confused with 'diction': and our first need is to clarify the difference between these two.

'Articulation' comes from the Latin word meaning 'to move by art or skill', and this is still its general meaning, sometimes referring to the jointed movement of, say, an armadillo — or a tractor-trailer. But it has come specifically to refer to the movement of the muscles of the lips, tongue, soft palate and jaw, in the act of speaking. It is these muscles which modify the sound produced by our breath as it vibrates through our larynx, and shape it into comprehensible speech.

'Diction' comes from the Latin word for 'say', and originally refers simply to the act of 'saying'. Obviously good 'diction' is impossible without effective 'articulation' — but whereas 'articulation' refers to the mechanical functions of the articulating muscles, 'diction' is more concerned with the effect of the speech on the audience. Good diction means clarity of utterance, including not only the clear articulation of words but the effective interpretation of text, the control of tone, resonance and phrasing, of colour and pitch and volume, of rhythm and stress, and also the ability to project speech to all corners of the theatre. We shall be returning to this subject in Chapter VI.

Articulation, then, is a mechanical function. When we speak, the muscles in and around the mouth pull and stretch. They press and curve with the dexterity of a very complicated machine, operating against each other or against the teeth and the hard palate. The breath that travels up into the mouth from the lungs carries sound from the larynx. It is this sounding breath which either comes out as 'vowel' sound — modified only by the shape of the lips and the position of the tongue; or as 'consonant' sound — getting interrupted, squeezed, channelled and buffered by the articulators, before being finally released into the air.

Mechanical? Machine? Yes, in a real sense these words are appropriate to describe the way that articulation works. But there is an obvious danger in thinking of our own speaking apparatus as a machine, as a mechanical function. If when we speak we become too hung up about the precisely correct placement of tongue-tip against teeth, or the exact shape of the lips, we shall find ourselves mesmerized by the mechanics, and less and less able to express ourselves meaningfully. It is like a pianist who becomes so pre-occupied with the mechanical operation of his fingers on the notes, that he can no longer play with feeling or even intelligence.

Many people fall into the trap of 'mechanical' thinking about the voice, and the student tries dutifully to become a perfect machine, given exercises which are designed to develop a good voice but which can lead to very different results. I remember my first class with one young singer-actor who I suddenly noticed was continually tensing his neck tendons until they protruded out almost to his earlobes. I asked him what he thought he was doing, and he told me cheerfully that his teacher had given him a series of exercises to strengthen his vocal cords "so that he could sing like Pavarotti". These exercises involved repeated tensing and relaxing of the neck and throat muscles: it was the Charles Atlas theory of 'dynamic tension' applied to the voice. His voice, we later discovered, was already damaged — he was permanently hoarse, and the voice cracked in its upper register. It is hard to imagine how a teacher could have had such an idea. What we have learned in our own earlier exercises has, I hope, made clear that relaxation is the key to healthy voice use. It is the feelings that must direct the contraction and relaxation of muscles, and strength must come not from technical labour but from exercising the desire to communicate. The moment any of our vocal work is carried out without breath/feeling connection, we are cutting the voice off from the roots of its primal function as a tool for the expression of our feelngs.

You are aware from our past exercises how feeling affects your breathing and the quality of breath determines the sound. As we start out on our articulation exercises, therefore, let us never be too stuck on the 'machine' of our articulating organs. Let us think of them not just as muscular and bony parts of the body but also as 'feeling places', which respond freely to the messages of our emotions.

Time for our first exercise. We need to apply to our articulators the same principles of relaxation and centering that we worked with earlier in relation to the body as a whole. And we need to become aware of these parts of ourselves in the same image-making way that we have been exploring since the first chapter.

Sit comfortably, your head 'floating' above the neck, and let your mouth and jaw relax, the lips slightly parted. Now imagine the tongue as a long, long, green leaf, which ends at the tip, but which starts somewhere far, far down, below your navel. In your imagination observe the qualities of your leaf: see its roots in the dark chambers of your centre. See it thrusting up, up, through your body tissue, ribs, neck and throat, into your mouth. We tend to think of leaves as passive, rustling in the wind. But have you ever seen a speeded-up film of plant life? The leaves coil and twist, swelling and reaching as they grow, seeking the light and the moisture. Capture this dynamic life-energy in the leaf of your tongue.

Now get this leaf to explore the world around it, the world of your mouth. As it brushes against your teeth, gums, the hard palate, the soft inside of your cheeks, your lips, let it register the different textures: smooth and rough, hard and soft, sharp and rounded. What are these things that the leaf discovers? Picture it in its own natural environment. Allow time for these experiences to register. And never forget that as you register each sensation, its message reaches back to the roots of the leaf, to your centre.

Rest.

Do you understand what we have done? We have explored our 'articulators' as sensed by the most active articulator — the tongue. We have done it through the use of an organic, non-mechanical image — an image which has emotional power. And we have motivated the actions of the muscles within that image's context.

The 'Leaf' Exercise helps us to become aware of our articulators' existence. Now let us concentrate on each of them in turn, using the images of this first exercise.

Take up the same position as for the previous exercise. Become conscious of your lips: where they are, how they feel. See them facing each other across the open mouth, and joined at the corners.

Now create the image of your lips as a flower. Within the context of this image, sense the living tissue in them, and the muscles around them which change their shape. Find an image for those muscles.

Let your upper lip explore the lower lip, and then vice versa. Roll the lips back over the teeth, and from side to side: first one lip, then the other. Close them now, first gently, then pucker them up, as in the kissing position. Holding them there, open and close them, imagining them as a rosebud opening to the light, and closing again.

Spend about two minutes on this exploration. And now, for about two minutes at a time, continue on your own to develop your awareness of other articulators in the following exercises.

THE TREES   EXERCISE IV.3

Create the image of your teeth as trees, the root of each tooth reaching down into the jawbone, like the root of a tree searching for nourishment. Feel the life in the trees, the sap that shapes them, the nerve that runs through them giving them consciousness and feeling. Become conscious of the feeling within them. Now run the great leaf of your tongue along them, first top and then bottom, stopping at each tooth, finding its separate shape and identity. Open them, close them, slide them against each other, explore the limits of their mobility.

THE SKY   EXERCISE IV.4

Create the image of the hard palate as the sky, and feel that the leaf of your tongue can actually touch the sky. So high up is the sky that your leaf will never be able to reach all of it. But where does the leaf actually come in contact with the sky? Feel the different areas: the tongue-tip, the middle, or the back, and explore the contact of each in turn. As the leaf touches the sky, the crack of thunder is heard. Make the sound. Dah – dah – dah... Do it quickly, sharply. Feel the thunder-crack reverberate through your skull.

Place the leaf of your tongue on the ridge of gum behind the upper front teeth: the rim of the sky, where the sky meets the trees. Explore the ridge.

Now push your tongue towards the back of your mouth, feeling where the hard palate becomes soft. Remember it.

THE CAVE

We go to the end of the sky and we come to marshy land: the soft palate — entrance to the cave that leads to the open throat. Let the back of your tongue/leaf roll around the entrance, feeling the soft texture of its surface. As it makes contact, release breath through the contact: kah – kah – kah.

THE TURNING OF THE WORLD

Imagine the world you have made as wanting to find more light in which to grow. Press the leaf of your tongue downwards against the floor of your mouth, the 'earth', and allow it to open the mouth wide, so that the lower jaw hangs down. Light floods into the world.

Now imagine the jaw as the bringer of light and darkness, of day and night. Slowly close the lower jaw, imaging the day turning to dusk, and the dusk to nightfall. Then slowly open it, imaging dawn breaking, the sunrise, and the arrival of day. See the light breaking over the leaf, the sky, the earth, the trees, the marshy land leading to the cave. Create the passing of several days and nights.

Finally, bring forth all these images, all these articulators, as if they are leaves and flowers being fed continual energy by the stream of life coming from your roots, from your centre. And imagine each of them as part of the network of your nervous system. You have seen the veins of a leaf: see that same network in all these bodily parts, bringing messages, sending messages back, in and out. Move them, stretch and squeeze them against one another.

And now let the leaf of your tongue REST on the floor of the world you have made. It is calm and still — but alive and ready now to draw on the imaginary life you have created for it.

Rest.

So these are the articulators. You have become aware of them through these exercises, and now we must put them to work. What do the articulators articulate?

The Articulators at Work: Consonants & Vowels

The job of articulation is to connect the dynamic, physical energy of our work as we press our breathstream around and through our articulating organs, with the rest of our bodies, with our feelings and our imaginations, and with our need to express and communicate.

The confrontation between the mechanical and the feeling in speech is an old difficulty. One of the people in modern times who have developed theories about it is Rudolf Steiner (1861-1925), the Austrian founder of 'anthroposophy', and the inspiration behind the hundreds of Steiner schools (usually called 'Waldorf' schools) set up around the world. Steiner wrote and taught about many aspects of life. He was a scholar of Goethe and worked to develop a science of religion and metaphysics. One of his most influential inventions was the practice of 'eurythmy', a language of gesture which he described as "the science of visible speech." Steiner created for each letter of the alphabet a physical gesture of the hands and arms, aiming to try and neutralize the inhibiting effect of the intellect. He described all these gestures put together as a kind of map of man's spiritual body, containing within it "the forces of growth, of nourishment and of memory."[22]

Steiner's theories have been taken hold of by a lot of enthusiastic and sometimes fanatical disciples. Other people have been very sceptical of what he said and thought. Steiner's eurythmic principles were the fashion in the 1910's and 1920's, and were practised in many schools in Europe and North America. The fashion has passed now, but some of Steiner's principles can still be seen working in many modern approaches to speech and to gesture and dance. It is interesting that Michael Chekhov, nephew of the great playwright Anton Chekhov, and one of the foremost acting teachers of 1920-50, wrote this in his book *Lessons for the Professional Actor*:

"The voice is a special thing and....the method we use in our school, that of Dr. Rudolf Steiner, is a very interesting and profound one, and also the results are not immediately obvious, and this is very good. When the results are there, they are of such a kind that our voice becomes a fine instrument for expressing and conveying the most subtle psychological things."[23]

For Steiner, human action in the world can be seen on three levels: WILLING, FEELING and THINKING. The human body, upright, expresses these three modes of existence. The feet planted on the ground represent the stability of the WILL. The hands and arms in their gestures represent the FEELINGS, expressing the language of the soul; while the head expresses the spirit and the THINKING element of the process. The three categories together create a channel, Steiner believed, for the expression of the actual 'being' of a person, and not just the image or sign of them.

It would be wrong to take a student of acting down the long and complicated path of Steiner's philosophy: anyone who wishes to, may explore it in spare time. But Steiner's approach to the sounds of language are a way of finding the life of the sounds of speech, and as such are of great value for any actor. The exercises later in this chapter are based on the ideas of Steiner, but they interpret him freely, in a way which I have found to be of maximum effectiveness.

This raises two points which need to be cleared up, because they are often a source of confusion to students. First, when Steiner began his studies of language and expression at the end of the last century, he naturally based his work on the German language, and the sounds he isolated and analysed, consonants and vowels, were the sounds of German, which do not always translate exactly into the sounds of other languages. His English-language disciples, always anxious to be accurate to the words of the master, have usually given his examples in the original German, followed by an English version: but we sometimes seem to be losing Steiner's ideas in the process — and when Steiner talks about German sounds as though they are universal, he does not always take these language differences into account.

Second, and more importantly, Steiner based his approach to speech sounds almost entirely on the letters of the alphabet. But of course these letters do not exactly correspond to speech sounds. English, in particular, is highly inconsistent in its spelling: 'car' and 'king', for example, start with the same sound, but the sound is spelt with different letters. Where our alphabet lists 21 consonants and 5 vowels (with 'y' sometimes serving as a sixth vowel), the phonetic alphabet for English lists 25 consonantal sounds and nineteen vowel sounds — a total of 44 different sounds.

Any work on speech sounds, therefore, should ideally be based not on the 26 letters of the (English) alphabet but on the 44 so-called 'phonemes' of the English/American phonetic alphabet, using the symbols standardized by the International Phonetic Association (I.P.A.). Unfortunately, these symbols, and the list of the sounds they symbolize, are not part of the general knowledge of ordinary people. The alphabet, on the other hand, has been familiar to us as long as we have known how to read and write, and carries with it a whole cargo of emotional associations. We have all known as children the way we used to give personalities, characters and even sexes to the different

So To Speak

letters. We know the list of them by heart as well as we know our own names. This familiarity makes them a rich source of formative imagery — something which the phonetic symbols cannot possibly arouse. Because of this, my exercises will also be based on the traditional alphabet, A to Z. As we explore each letter we will of course try and extend our sense of it to cover all its sounds and uses.

As we have already seen, language is made up of two kinds of sounds — VOWELS, which are made on the breath, and CONSO-NANTS, which are made by interrupting the breath. The articulators do play a part in the shaping of the vowels — especially the lips and jaw, which take up the various positions necessary to make the sounds of "ah," "oh," "ee," "oo" etc. Let us concentrate first on the formation of consonants, because this is where the articulators do their most energetic and complicated work. We will then move to the vowels.

First, the Consonants:

Consonants are usually divided into six different groups, according to the way they interrupt the breath:

1. PLOSIVES are sounds you make by blocking off the breath entirely for a brief period of time, and building up air pressure behind the blockage. You then suddenly 'explode' the air to produce the sound. The first sound in 'ball' or 'pinch' is plosive.

2. FRICATIVES are different from plosives in that you do not have to block the breath so completely. You just need a small opening through which you release the breath. The first sound in the words 'free' or 'save' is fricative.

3. GLIDES are consonant sounds you make by moving your articulators from one position to another — WHILE MAKING THE SOUND. The first sound in the word 'yellow' is a glide. Say the 'y' sound slowly and you will hear it gliding, and feel the mouth and tongue moving to make the sound.

4. NASALS — as you would guess from the name — are made by blocking off the mouth with lips or with parts of the tongue, so that the breath goes out of the nostrils. The letters 'm' and 'n' are nasals — so is the compound 'ng'. You cannot say these sounds without some of the sound vibrating in the nasal passage.

5. LATERAL sounds are produced by dropping the sides of the tongue and releasing the air through the sides of the mouth. The first and last sounds in the word 'loll' are laterals. 'L' is the only lateral consonant in English.

6. AFFRICATES are combinations of plosives and fricatives. There are only two in English: they are the sounds at the beginning and end of the word 'charge'.

So To Speak

Most books of speech will go on to describe exactly how to make each consonant sound. Here is an example:

"THE CONSONANTS [t] AS IN [tim] team AND [d] AS IN [dim] deem

These two sounds are known as post-dentals, or lingua-alveolar plosives. In their production the tip of the tongue makes contact with the gum ridge just above the upper teeth in front...As in the case of [p], one should avoid an exaggerated, too-noisy aspiration of breath in sounding [t]. On the other hand, omission or excessive diminution of the aspiration will make [t] resemble [d], and the speech will sound foreign.."[24]

As a description this is an accurate account of what happens when we make the sounds of 't' and 'd', but knowledge of the precise muscular actions required to form a sound does not lead automatically to clear articulation of that sound. In fact, too much consciousness of the mechanical operation of articulating a sound, as I have already tried to show, can very easily get in the way of our ability to communicate feeling and ideas through it. Our attention, instead of turning outside towards the hearer, turns in on itself. And if language is not communicating, it is not language.

The following exercises, then, are designed to awaken our emotional relationship with sounds of speech, and with the alphabet which (however imperfectly) symbolizes those sounds. By creating an emotional and 'lived-through' experience in connection with each letter, we find ourselves enacting sound with our whole body, and combining thinking, feeling and action in a single unit of experience and awareness.

Remove any tight clothes you may be wearing, and then lie down on the floor. Feel your body melting into the floor, letting go of tension and stress in ways which are now becoming familiar for us.

Now, begin listening to some music (I often use Pachabel's "Canon"). Once the music is flowing over you, begin to try sensing it not just with your ears but with your senses of touch, taste, smell, and sight. Try in other words to listen to it WITH YOUR ENTIRE BODY.

(This is not a metaphor for what we are doing, but the actual experience — music and all sound comes through the air in waves, which flow all over us, subtly interacting with the frequencies around our bodies, and with our hair follicles, which are particularly sensitive. Do you recall what happens to you when a teacher scrapes chalk across a blackboard? You don't just hear it with your ears — your whole body reacts and shivers at the sound.)

So, let the music flow around and through you, caressing your body, playing itself through you until it becomes a part of you. Feel the colours and textures, the flavour of the music, its smells, its taste, its touch, its heat and cold, its light and dark, so that all your senses combine to receive the music to the fullest possible extent.

At the end of the music, rest still. If images or words have arisen from the music, allow them to dance to your memory of the music's patterns and rhythms.

Now slowly rise to your feet, and, with the same music playing another time, move your body to it, creating shapes that may have been evoked by the music. THINK OF YOUR MOVING AS ANOTHER WAY OF LISTENING.

RIDING THE SOUND WAVES   EXERCISE IV.9

Face your partner, and with the music playing a third time, imagine the sound waves filling the space between you. Ride on those waves with your body movements, creating shapes and patterns like a dolphin in the sea, and communicate with one another through these patterns and shapes. (If you have no partner, imagine one.)

SILENT MUSIC   EXERCISE IV.10

With the music now silent, continue moving to it, imagining the sound as it plays in your memory.

Rest.

Now we are ready for our exploration of the form and the sounds of language, dealing first with consonants.

Find a space to be in the room on your own.

Then, still hearing the music in your inner ear, begin by creating a gesture or movement for the sound of 'b'. As you make the gesture, whisper the sound to yourself. Become aware of the air being blocked and then released by the lips: find a movement and gesture which unite with that whispered sound.

You can, if you like, draw ideas from the very written shape of the letter: but be aware of the danger of simply imitating a literal shape — and becoming a kind of printing press in the air. The shape of the signs that we use for each letter, after all, are probably not originally designed to be an image of the sound (though maybe some are — does the letter 'o' not represent the shape taken by the mouth when speaking "o"?).

Try to feel the space between the sound and the shape you are making with your movement. You are living the sound. Your whole body is articulating it. Try to remember the shape you have created for 'b'. Give it a clear beginning and end.

Move to the letter 'c', giving it the same care and conscious attention, and only leaving it when you have found a similar gesture and shape which seems to you to articulate the essence of the sound; a gesture which when you think of it is part of the sound.

Work at your own pace through the consonants of the alphabet, giving each one the same absolute conscious focus, exploring the essence of the sound and the way it is made, and using your free imagination to find the gesture which articulates that sound. Rest when you wish. Above all, never hurry. Never let the progress through the sounds become something done by rote — stop and rest if you find yourself losing focus, and use the rest-time to go over in your memory the sound-gestures you have already fashioned.

When all the consonants have their shape and gesture, take a further rest. Then, without pause, work from the beginning to the end of your sequence of sound-gestures, still carefully defining the beginnings and ends of each, but now merging smoothly and without pause from one to the next.

This long and concentrated exercise may be spread over more than one session. But you will be surprised at how much of your sequence you will remember, if you have really concentrated while creating it. And when the sequence of sounds is done, you will possess a living memory bank of physicalized sound — something that will enrich every syllable you ever speak. Do you understand this? Let me put it another way:

One problem with language is that we learn it so early that our way of speaking becomes 'second nature'. The work of the actor is to bring this 'second nature,' the habitual way of speaking, back into the conscious mind, and to give each sound he or she may utter a new life, a new sparkle. The gesture for each sound actually 'reifies' the sound — actualizes it. In doing this exercise we pull those consonants out of the daily stream of language, and give each of them their own physical life, a gesture which extends the sound's impact, creates for it a physical sense memory as well as a sound memory. Then, when we return to the business of speaking, we find that each movement of our articulators, each sound we make, has a new contour, a new life, a new physical resonance, with the memory of a specific physical gesture coded not only in our articulators but in the muscles and bones of our body. 'Second nature' has become — first nature? Something like that!

It's the first time I realized that the sounds have their own kind of chemistry — almost like a force of their own, independent of me."

A Student

And Now, The Vowels:

In Chapter II we explored breathing, the basic act of a living creature, and also the energy source for vocal utterance. A vowel, sound, as we have seen, is simply a modification of the voiced breath as it is exhaled. The voiced breath is not interrupted as in the consonant, but its sound is modified by adjusting the position of the tongue, lips, teeth and soft palate. Make the sound 'ah'— then make the sound 'oh' — and then the sound 'ee'. It is as though vowels are painted on to the breath, the breathstream being the basic element, the canvas.

Speech, then, is made up of 'painted' breathstream (vowels), and of interruptions to that breathstream (consonants). When we speak, the more clearly we articulate the different sounds of speech, the more easily the listener can understand. This is clearly true of consonants. But it also true of vowels. 'Road', 'rod', 'reed', 'red' and 'rid', all meaning very different things, differ from each other in sound only by their vowel sounds; each of them requiring a different position of the articulators. Anyone who wishes to be understood — and actors above all — must be able to form these sounds clearly and distinctly, giving each vowel not only its distinct colour, but also sufficient length of time for the listener's ear to be able to identify it. This 'length' is sometimes referred to as 'quantity'.

There are five vowel symbols in the English alphabet: 'a', 'e', 'i', 'o', 'u'. But, as I have already pointed out, this is not a list of the vowel sounds of the spoken language, which consist of sixteen different vowel sounds, and three vowel 'blends', referred to as 'diphthongs'. Any standard text will list these phonemes, and will contain many drills that the actor can practise in order to improve skill and dexterity.[25]

But the formation of vowel sounds has meant very different things to people who have concerned themselves with the art of speech and acting. Rudolf Steiner wrote about the sound 'ah':

"When we utter the sound 'ah' we feel, if our instinct is at all healthy, that this sound really proceeds from our inmost being when we are in a state of wonder and amazement....When man utters the sound 'ah' he sends forth out of himself a part of his own being, namely the quality of wonder. This he imprints into the air...Philosophy, love of wisdom begins with 'ah'.... 'Ah' corresponds to man in his highest perfection. Thus 'ah' is man, and in the sound we are expressing something which is felt in the depths of the human soul."[26]

Not many these days would make such intense claims for one simple vowel sound. Michael Chekhov's belief in Steiner's approach was rare even in the 1940's and 50's. But Stanislavsky, the most respected acting theorist of our century, also understood the need to regard vowels — and consonants — from an emotional and even spiritual point of view. He quotes approvingly from his own teacher Tortsov:

"Do you not realize that an inner feeling is released through the clear sound of the A (ah)? The sound is bound up with certain deep inner experiences which seek release and easily float out from the recesses of one's bosom. But there is another A sound. It is dull, muffled, does not float out easily, but remains inside to rumble ominously — as if in some cavern or vault. There is also the insidious AAA which whirls out to drill its way into the person who hears it. The joyous A sound rises from one like a rocket, in contrast to the ponderous A which, like an iron weight, sinks into the bottom of one's wellsprings."[27]

Whereas Steiner treats the vowel sound as though it is a particle of elemental matter, a divine spark, Stanislavsky (Tortsov) concentrates more on the variety of ways in which the vowel sound can be used in expressing a range of different feelings. But while both are interested in clarity of articulation, neither of them start with diagrams of the muscles of the articulators, or descriptions of the position of the tongue. Instead, they both conjure up images which grab our imagination, and make us feel as though we have truly experienced the sound of which they speak.

Let us then end this long chapter with a group of exercises dealing with the vowels. Because vowel sounds are 'painted' on the breathstream, the production of that breathstream from our centre (solar plexus) is of major importance to the formation of vowels. Let us start with a 'toning' exercise, to prepare the body instrument.

1. Lie on the floor (in a circle if you are in a group), and with closed eyes spend a few minutes in 'central' or 'colour' breathing (see Exercises in Chapter II).

2. Keeping the eyes closed, chant the sound of 'ah' (as in 'calm') with full breath, nine separate times, sustaining the sound until the lungs are empty. Do not force the sound, and do not strain at the end of the breath. Each sound will last at least seven seconds.

3. Do the same, nine times, with each of the following sounds: 'ee' (as in 'sea'); 'oh' (as in 'so'); 'uu' (as in 'blue').

With each vowel sound, imagine the vowel-sound as a stream issuing from your centre. Visualize the shape and colour of the stream as it flows, imagining — or letting emerge — a different colour and shape for each of the sounds. If colours change, go with them. Explore the change. Always visualize the stream coming from the source, the centre of your body.

When you have completed the cycle of nine for each of the four sounds, be silent for a moment. Can you still hear the sounds you have been making? What sensations is your body feeling now? Have they come as a result of your chanting? Is there any difference in the way you feel from when you began the exercise? Be aware of these subtle differences because they are the actor's real tools.

You have explored a sequence of separate sounds. Now you create a 'kaleidoscope:'

4. On one breath, start with 'ah', and then slowly move through the other three sounds: 'aaaaaa-eeeeeee-ooooooo-uuuuuuuu'. Now let images of colour and shape come of their own volition — as I sometimes say to students, "Look into the dark space behind your eyes, and see what emerges". Play freely with images, and as you do so, play too with the pitch of the sound you make. Let it rise and fall. Explore the

Articulation   85

feelings the different pitches arouse.

This exercise will take at least fifteen minutes and can extend as long as forty. The tempo is steady and reflective. Any hurry will take away from the value of what you are doing. When you feel that your exploration is complete, rest in silence (a group often finds that it ends at almost exactly the same moment). As you rest, observe with your ears. What do you hear? Can you still hear the essential difference between the different vowel sounds? Can they tell you their nature?

When you get up and leave the room, you may be a little dizzy. But you will almost certainly find a change in your speech, in your posture and way of walking, and in the way you see things.

NOW WE ARE READY TO EXPLORE THE GESTURES WHICH CAN BRING THE VOWELS TO LIFE.

ATTITUDE & SOUND   EXERCISE IV.13

Because the vowels are 'painted' breathstream, the speaking of vowels is like uttering some of the basic cries of life, as we respond to the world around us.

Stand relaxed and loose. If you are in a group, stand in a circle, leaving plenty of space between you.

Say 'ah', letting the sound extend for several seconds. Repeat it with more and more energy. It is a cry of wonder, of realization. Now, as you utter the sound, raise the arms, reaching up to the sky, as though responding with wonder and amazement to the world before you. THE GESTURE IS THE EXPRESSION OF THE SOUND.

Now be silent, but remain with your arms outstretched, reaching up, palms forward. Imagine the forces of the universe streaming through your arms. Become conscious of the gesture your arms are making, and the wonder and amazement that it signifies. And when you are ready, express that meaning with the sound 'ah'. THE SOUND IS THE EXPRESSION OF THE GESTURE.

Pause.

Say 'ee', letting the sound extend for several seconds. Repeat it with more and more energy.

Now pause and raise your arms as in the 'ah' gesture of wonder. Then imagine that you are taking the energy of the universe and drawing it into your heart. Draw the arms down and cross them over your chest, each hand resting on its opposite shoulder. As the gesture is completing, repeat the sound 'ee'.

Think of 'ee' as the sound you make when something has happened, and you are feeling its effects —— 'ee'... 'ee'... Repeat the sound, each time returning to the 'ah' position, and then drawing the arms down across the chest as before. And each time, bring the experience into your chest — 'take it on the chest'— embrace it and 'deal with it'.

So we have wonder, 'ah,' and we have response to an outer stimulus, 'ee.' Now pause again, and then:

Say 'i' (eye), letting the sound extend for several seconds. Repeat with mounting energy.

Pause, and take up the position for 'ee'. Then release the hands, and make the gesture of opening out your arms until they are stretched wide on each side of your body. With the gesture, say again: 'i'. Return to the chest position, and make the sound and gesture of 'i' several times.

The stream of energy has its source starting from the heart, and flowing out through the arms and legs. Link the assertion of your self with the gesture. Think of 'i' as 'I', 'I myself', and the expanding gesture as the affirmation of the fact that you exist and are a force. Pause.

Say 'oh', letting the sound extend as before. Repeat it several times as before, with more and more energy and power.

Then pause, and take up the position for 'i'. Now raise the arms from their positions stretched out on each side of your body — raise them until they form a half circle around your head, the hands with palms inward and fingers of one hand pointing towards the fingers of the other, not quite touching. As you make the gesture say again 'oh'.

Think of the 'oh' gesture as neither reaching nor grasping. It is a decorative pattern, a circle, conveying our oneness with the world. The world is in your arms, the world is your arms. You become the world.

Repeat the gesture and the sound several times, encouraging your imagination to feel this sense of oneness with the universe. Pause.
Say 'u' (oo), letting the sound extend. Repeat the sound with increasing power.

Pause, and take up the position of 'oh'. Then draw the arms down, and cross them, the left hand resting on the right biceps, and the right hand cupping the left elbow. As you make the gesture, repeat the sound 'u'.

Think of 'u' as a feeling of returning to yourself, of being restored to your stillness, to your own small space in the world. It is not a shrinking gesture, but a release from striving. Repeat slowly, always with this image clear in your mind. Then pause.

Remind yourself, in your own time, of each gesture. And then — in your own time — enact the gestures and sounds in continuous sequence, always remembering and re-enacting in your mind the specific psychological gesture that we have attributed to each sound. Do not blur the sounds and gestures; finish one before moving to the next. The psychological gestures or attitudes that go with the sounds are also a sequence — the shape of a day, or a life.

If you catch yourself imitating the sounds and gestures rather than experiencing them, you should stop, think and then start again.

Anybody who finds themselves forgetting the sequence, and looking at others in the group in order to recall something, is clearly not experiencing. Do not look at others!

When you have completed the sequence several times, rest.

Summary

From these exercises in articulation, the actor gains a body of experience in relation to his/her voice and utterance — a set of images and sense memories. These can be remembered and referred back to, enriching the sense of consciousness in speaking, and building the confidence of the actor in knowledge of the vocal instrument and of the way it produces comprehensible sound. Above all, this body of experience can connect and re-connect the voice with the feelings, with the imaginative power, even with what Steiner calls the 'soul,' so that speech really does function as a 'visible' expression of the whole person — the willing, feeling, thinking person — what we are when we are living at the full extent of our potential. Clearly nothing is more valuable for an actor — who must become many people in the course of a life in the acting art — than to be able to express the wholeness of a character's identity in a way which communicates that identity to others.

One of you now sits, and the other, standing behind, massages the neck and shoulders...(p.105)

V.
Text

In the first four chapters we have concentrated on posture, breathing, relaxation and articulation. The exercises we have been doing have been designed to help us to know our physical selves — to understand what it is we are working with. Now it is time to approach a piece of dramatic text.

But just a minute — what about 'Diction?' Don't we have to learn about things like phrasing, inflection, emphasis and rhythm, before we actually deal with a text?

Good question, as the saying goes. But in the end, diction is only 'good' if it expresses (from the Latin meaning 'pushes out') what lies in the words that are being spoken. And to be able to do this — or even to practise it — we must have some words to work with. This is why we are dealing with text now, and why I have placed our chapter on 'Diction' at the end.

We have, in fact, reached the point where speech and acting meet — the point where everything that has been learned about relating the voice to the body and to the feelings has to be put to the service of an acting experience. It is at this point that speech teachers often get into trouble. I remember the problems at the Stratford Festival in Canada, when a teacher suggested to a young actor a 'reading' for a certain line. At the next rehearsal the director asked testily "Why are you saying the line like that?" The voice teacher was rebuked for overstepping her bounds.

The difficulty is that there are no bounds. There is no clearly marked boundary where the voice finishes and the complete actor takes over. In fact the whole idea of our exercises has been to break down whatever barriers might exist between the various areas of acting craft. Learning how to speak lines of text is only one part of the actor's job. The speaking must coordinate with the moving, both must be linked to the mind and heart, and everything must be rooted in a single source — the actor's centre.

Voice work, as we have said, is like practising scales for a pianist — in the end an expressive 'technique' must be learned so well that it becomes second nature to us. Or it is like driving a car: the beginner must search around for the gears and the pedals, but an experienced driver can drive without thinking about it — and so concentrate on where he/she is going. The text is the goal for which the actor's voice is prepared. Let us then leave our voice work on one side for the moment, and spend a little time looking at various approaches to 'text' in theatre situations. I will then be describing some exercises which can help us approach a piece of text — with the same reliance on our physical and emotional inner world as we have been developing in our work up to now.

Because our theatre, the theatre of western culture, is normally based on a pre-written script, one of the most important areas of craft for our actors is the job of bringing words on a page to life on the stage. Every theatre school has classes on text analysis to help actors develop this area of expertise. And when they join us in the profession, young actors will find that most rehearsal periods in the theatre begin (after a talk by the director, in which he or she sets out the approach that is being taken) with a reading of the text, slow and careful, sitting round a table, analysing what characters mean by what they say, and what the playwright means by it all. We also study social history and background, problems of class and style and relationships, and gradually out of this work — which we do both individually in our 'homework' and together as a company — we put together a picture of the play. We then rehearse, each of us working on our own characters, both in themselves and in relation to the people around them within the play's situations.

Along the way we have a lot of talk about the psychological goings-on inside the mind of each character. Freud has revolutionized our understanding of acting, of course, giving us some important clues about the difference between conscious, visible behaviour, and subconscious drives and obsessions. An actor these days has to be a good amateur psychologist in order to hold his/her own in these discussions.

So To Speak

The danger in this very sensible approach is that we start out as scholars and then turn ourselves into actors: the first encounter with the text is as a critic — or even as a psychiatrist. But this is not how we approach life. We are in life from the start, and every moment! We can't look at it from the sidelines and then plunge in when we know what is going on and are ready to deal with it. Theatre is of course not life — but is it not supposed to "hold a mirror up to nature"?[27]

Anyway, to try and break down the distancing effect of this kind of literary, historical and psychological study — to get away from the potential stuffiness of 'literary' theatre — a number of techniques have been developed to help find the life-force, the emotional or physical energy that lies behind a sequence of words in the text.

For example, directors these days will ask actors in the early stages of rehearsal to improvize scenes — doing one of the scenes already in the play but in the actors' own words ('paraphrasing' the scene); or sometimes playing a scene which is only imagined or implied in the text, such as a childhood memory recalled by an adult character. Sometimes an actor is asked to select the animal that seems to embody their character, and to improvize the animal's movements, reactions and vocal utterances within the context of the play. Sometimes an actor may be called on to mime a scene, in order to transfer expressiveness from words to actions. All these methods can be effective in the job of breaking down the literariness or wordiness of the initial approach, and finding the physical or pre-verbal impulses of the characters.[28]

A performance I saw some years ago took this technique considerably further. The production was still based on a text, *Blood Wedding* by Federico Garcia Lorca, but the director did not undertake the usual business of 'blocking' the staging. He allowed the actors to improvize their relationships, their tone of speech and speed of delivery; their motivations and even their moves — this approach even carrying through into performance. The actors were encouraged to think things through differently every night, so that every performance was different and had its own 'reality'.

The Director's Note in the program was heart-warming: "A director should be neither a dictator, however benign, nor an ultimate authority. He should be a stimulator, an encourager, a coach, an arbitrator...The process is to uncover, together, layer by layer, the clues that will reveal the world of the play... The actors, instead of being forced to justify pre-ordained results — which are static — are encouraged to pursue a network of open-ended drives, needs, purposes, deeds — which are active. An external structure (rigid, closed) is replaced by an internal structure (flexible, open). That is to say, the structure is created within the actor. The actors gain not only greater creative freedom, but also greater responsibility..."

How wonderful it was to read these words. The play, when I saw it, was not tremendously interesting — not that night, at least — but the process seemed to be on exactly the right track. But then afterwards I met one of the principal members of the company, an actress of many years experience and an old friend. From her I learned another side of the story: in her view the director had created a really wretched experience for the company of actors, diminishing them at every opportunity, never satisfied, never once encouraging them in the difficult process he had inflicted upon them. Of course, human nature being what it is, everyone worked doubly hard to try to earn his praise — but he only scorned them more. Everyone who attempted to make use of something from their experience was accused of falling back on old habits. Some of the younger actors even began behaving in the most excessive way in order to show their commitment to the process, bullying and menacing the other actors. The rehearsal was a hell on earth. So much for the director's idealism!

The approaches I have described here are all ways of dealing with a pre-written text, and each of them in their own way attempts to make the text 'live', to make it 'real', using various methods for achieving this. The goal is, really, to have the finished performance appear to have no text at all — as if everything is simply made up as it goes along. This is the true aim of 'naturalism' — the actor appears to 'be' the character, and the character speaks words which appear to be not the playwright's but his/her own.

But there are also dramatic projects which get away completely from a pre-written text. I have been involved with several: and one particularly is worth remembering because it had a profound effect on me and on my ideas of theatre, and is relevant to this discussion.

I was once invited to join a small company of actors at the studio theatre of the National Arts Centre in Ottawa, Canada. It was at a time when fresh ideas were in the air throughout the theatre of North America. The director had been hired to run an 'experimental' theatre season, at this new but already rather stuffy institution, and he had decided to go for broke. We were to start by developing ourselves as an ensemble through exercises and improvizations, and out of this process our first production was to be created. There was to be no text, but the director had chosen a topic — the Spanish-American War of 1898. He had assembled a mass of documentary material, and we were to sort it out and shape it as a company. The director, who had already had some experience with creating script through improvization, had in fact come to a conclusion similar to the one held by our *Blood Wedding* friend: that the director should get out of the way. The difference was that he really did so. He also made it clear that that he would not make final decisions about the script — these too would have to be arrived at by the group as a whole.

In the early 'rehearsals' we were given a list of some of the major characters involved in the historical event, together with a brief biography, physical description, excerpts from speeches or writings, anecdotes etc., and each of us was allowed to choose the character he/she wished to play. Then 'encounters' were set up between characters — not necessarily encounters that could have taken place in real life — and we could begin to improvize our characters within these scenes. This was real actor's freedom, and I tell you it was a frightening business: we did not have much material to use, and often felt foolish being so completely exposed and having to press on with almost no idea of what we were doing or where we were going. In spite of all this, we were excited by what was happening and amazed by the things we found ourselves accomplishing.

The problem came when the advertized date of our first production drew near and we had still not created anything resembling a play. We looked to the director to take over — and in spite of the pressure the Centre was placing on him, he refused. In the end we voted democratically for him to create a set of rules within which our improvizations would take place. Of the twelve actors, three became 'caretakers' and were responsible for ensuring that the rules were adhered to. If anyone broke a rule, a whistle would blow and he or she could be interrogated and 'punished' — ostracised, buried up to the neck in

Text 95

sand, condemned to speak from then on in a certain way or to wear some garment. So the production was run like a game, with forty-five minutes allotted to each of the two acts, and a number of 'plays' (in the football sense) up our sleeves, but with no set order of events.

The final results were not exactly enjoyable either for the cast or the audience. But a few of us realized that something highly unusual was happening. Every time you 'went on' you had simply no idea what was going to happen, how you would be challenged, and whether you would be able to meet the challenge. And yet out there was an audience which had paid to see the performance and expected to be professionally entertained. Audiences who often complain that what they go to see is not very well done because it is not 'real', now tended to complain about something which was absolutely 'real'— everything they saw was really happening, and happening for the first time. Every time you spoke, you had to speak out of your own immediate responses — and somehow find ways of sensing and enhancing the drama, of making things happen. One critic slammed the piece, but returned a week later and wrote a surprising 'recantation,' saying how important the show was, how much he had learned — and how he admired the courage of the performers! I still run into people who saw the play and have not forgotten it.

From this haunting experience I learned for the first time to understand the feeling of genuine spontaneity on the stage: the difference between speaking a text and performing a text AS THOUGH creating it. I learned about courage, about the loneliness of responsibility but the comfort of being one of a group who were all in the same situation and all dealing with it as well as each of them could. Our own characters and personalities were challenged and naked — and our reactions of fear, amusement, anger, embarrassment, shame, contempt, gentleness, pride, sympathy and love were drawn out of us not by craft but by the sheer 'reality' of the situation, and the pressure it put on us to survive. Some of us didn't come out of the text very well: the stress even turned one or two of us into 'real' bastards. We seemed to have created our own prison, our own concentration camp — is this what all people do when they are not controlled by some authority? And yet with all its terrors I would not have missed it. It was the only genuinely un-directed play, the only true 'collective' I have ever been involved with. Too often, so-called collectives are in fact heavily dominated by a director who goes through the motions of democracy but in fact controls events with an iron hand.

From these different approaches we learn that there are a lot of ways in which to approach a play. I have spent some time describing them because the point where the actor has to apply his/her instincts, passions and intelligence to the process of creating and repeating learned and memorized text and gestures is so often the point where creative originality and authentic feeling dries up, replaced by 'technique.' Clever analysis and lots of careful pre-planning, in other words, has its dangers. Actors who have 'done their homework' can so easily look just like that — conscientious students who are bringing their teacher the fruits of their labour, and waiting expectantly for a good grade. It is not an easy business, and in the end of course the process does involve all the approaches that I have described, and others too. In whatever way it is achieved, an actor in the final performance must offer above all an immediate experience: he/she must appear to respond to situation as though there is no text but only an actual situation in place and time — the 'here and now' — with which the character must seem to cope on the spur of the moment and with no pre-thinking.

Actors, we all know, must be able to imagine that they are the character they are playing, and to forget who they are as actors — actors who like any other workers are counting the minutes to the break and wondering what's for dinner. But must this separation between character and actor be so complete? Is there a way in which we can graft our own self, our drives and needs, our ways of thinking and talking, on to our acted character? I believe there is. What I would like to offer now is an approach which I have found effective, especially as a process for performance in training. It is an initial approach to text which has developed partly from my 'collective' experience in Ottawa, but also from the speech work that we have already been exploring.

The Micro–Macro Approach

In the Renaissance, many philosophers made use of an ancient Cabbalistic concept whereby the cosmos was called 'macrocosm' (from the Greek meaning 'large cosmos'), and the human being was called the 'microcosm'('small cosmos'). They believed that on a small scale the human being reflected and reproduced in every detail the elements of the large cosmos — like the universe in miniature. Similarly everything else — all natural objects at every level of scale — was related up and down the spectrum of the cosmos. This idea, of the small object being a tiny version of the whole, meant that Renaissance studies of humanity and of the universe went hand in hand. The four elements of nature — earth, air, water, fire — were repeated for example, in various proportions in the physical body, thus affecting the 'humours' or temperament: sanguine, choleric, melancholy or phlegmatic.[29]

This belief in universal harmony and inter-relationships was abandoned with the scientific revolution, which threw out general principles about almost everything and started again with empirical experiments to test every piece of knowledge separately. The writer and cleric Thomas Sprat wrote about this at the time: "What we have gotten is sense," he remarked, "and we have lost a world of fine fabling."[30]

But in modern times we have begun to see the limits of scientific inquiry, and are starting to realize that Renaissance ideas of universal harmony and inter-connectedness were not so misguided after all. In the last thirty years the separate departments of scientific study have been starting to link up again, and finding that the universe really does repeat itself at all its levels. And so with humanity too: people's identity can now be determined by the print of a finger, a hair of their head or a drop of their blood.

The scientific method influenced a lot of other things besides science. In fact the conventional study of a text which we looked at at the beginning of this chapter could itself be described as 'scientific.' What I would like to suggest now is an approach which is more imaginative and less scientific; an approach which relies more on oneself than on the 'empirical' evidence of the text. In this approach a section of text is picked out and looked at and worked on in isolation from the rest of the play. We approach the selected fragment as though it is a microcosm of the whole: something we can play with and squeeze and knock around, in order to make it our own like a suit of clothes, or even something which we graft on to ourselves as a farmer grafts shoots on to a fruit tree. We can then use it — now become part of ourselves — as our personal entry into the play as a whole. In honour of our friends of the Renaissance, I have called this approach 'Micro–Macro.'

In the exercises that follow we cannot possibly expect to move through the complete process of dealing with an entire play. But I want to show how it is possible to make a fresh and original kind of beginning: a beginning which relies not on study but on ourselves, on what is happening here and now as we find ourselves — without preparation, without study — within a scene. From the work on this single scene, a strange kind of symbiosis with character can begin to take place. It is this living experience of one moment of the play that we can take with us as we build the rest of the play around it.

For these exercises we need a partner, and a scene with two characters, preferably of opposite sex. You can find your own passage if you wish, or you can use a scene that I enjoy working with, from Ibsen's *A Doll's House*. I have left out most stage directions, and am purposely not providing an introduction at this point.

From *A Doll's House* by Henrik Ibsen, Act Three. . .

TORVALD
Ah, Nora, there is something sweetly satisfying for a husband to know that he has forgiven his wife with his whole heart. It's as though she belongs to him twice over. It's as though he brings her into the world again. And now she is at once both wife and child. And that is what you shall be to me, my poor, bewildered little Nora. Never be frightened of anything again, Nora. Just open your heart to me. I shall be both your will and your conscience. — What's this? Aren't you coming to bed? You've changed.

NORA
Yes, Torvald, I have changed.

TORVALD
But why now? — so late?

NORA
I shall not sleep tonight.

TORVALD
But my dear Nora —

NORA
It isn't that late. Sit down, Torvald.

TORVALD
What does this mean?

NORA
Sit down. You and I have a lot to talk about.

TORVALD
You alarm me, Nora. I don't understand.

So To Speak

NORA

No, that's just it. You don't understand me. And I never understood you — until tonight. No, don't interrupt me. Just listen to what I have to say. You and I have some things to settle, Torvald.

TORVALD

What do you mean by that?

NORA

Does anything strike you about the way we are sitting here?

TORVALD

What?

NORA

We have been married for eight years. Does it occur to you that this is the first time you and I, as man and wife, have had a serious talk?

TORVALD

What do you mean, serious?

NORA

In eight years — no, more — ever since we first met — we have never exchanged one serious word — no, not one.

TORVALD

Did you expect me to drag you into all my business worries? Business you couldn't possibly have helped me with?

NORA

I'm not talking about business. What I am saying is that we have never sat down together and tried to get to the bottom of anything.

TORVALD

But, my dear Nora, what good would it do if we did?

NORA

That's just the point. You've never understood me. A great wrong has been done me, Torvald. First by Father, and then by you.

TORVALD

What? But we two have loved you more than anyone in the world!

NORA

You've never loved me. You just found it fun being in love with me.

TORVALD

Nora, how can you say that?

NORA

It's the truth. When I lived at home with Father, he fed me his opinions until they became my opinions. Or — if they didn't — I kept quiet about it, because he wouldn't have liked it. He called me his 'little doll', and he treated me just the way I treat my dolls. Then I came here to live in your house —

TORVALD

What a way to describe our marriage! . . .[31]

I have purposely picked a passage which does not end with a dramatic climax, and the first reaction of any actor who is not familiar with the play will be to want to know the rest of the scene, the rest of the play — and also what happened just before, which has led to this moment. All this will come. But for now let us go another way...

1. Decide between you which characters you want to play. Then read the scene once aloud, without preparation.

2. Don't discuss the scene at all after you have read it, but each of you immediately pick a phrase — or even a word — from the lines of your character. It can be any phrase, but try and pick one that has somehow attracted your attention: "Little doll" or "eight years" or "What does this mean?" or "a great wrong," or even "bed," or "two." Sit opposite your partner. Each close your eyes, and imagine the word or phrase, repeating itself silently in your head and body — do not speak it aloud. Now focus your concentration on it, and out of it conjure up images, pictures. If there is an object mentioned, try and see it. If it is an abstract phrase or word, try and apply it to someone or something concrete. Let "bed" be your bed at home — or any other bed. Apply "two" to all sorts of different things in pairs... Keep starting again, and imagining something else: allow pictures to come to the mind's eye, and let these pictures awaken memories, sensations, images, colours...

Finally, start to 'free-associate' — let your word or phrase give rise to another and another, with no necessary connection. Allow the random images to pile up: "Eight years"... eight chairs ... table ... dinner ... grandfather at dinner ... old men ... hearse ... flowers ... lilies ... white ... dress ... Let your mind go wherever it wants, and go with it.

3. Now, let me assume you have been successful in creating images and pictures and colours as I describe, and so have built up a little web of associations, direct and indirect, around the phrase/word you have picked. Now, with eyes still closed, you start speaking the word or phrase to your partner, and your partner replies with the word or phrase that he/she has been working with. Have a conversation using only these phrases/words. Say them with every different intonation you can imagine, listening to the tone of your partner and picking up on it and responding to it with your phrase. This is very important: it is a real personal inter-action, NOT two separate monologues. At any point you choose, during the conversation, open your eyes, continu-

ing while looking directly at your partner as much as you would if talking to someone.

You have only read the scene once. But it is likely that even in the one reading you will have picked up something of the relationship, and that the tone of this 'conversation' will reflect it.

4. Now repeat the exercise, choosing another phrase or word and going through each of the stages as before.

5. And now, pick up your text and read the scene again. Any difference from the first time? There has to be — there always is. But let's not stop here. Now, with your increased understanding of what is going on between the two characters, pick a third word or phrase which seems to you to be really significant to what is going on, and repeat our exercise once more with the new phrases — but this time speak the word/phrase directly to your partner, with eyes open from the start of the 'conversation.'

6. And now, once more, read the scene.

My experience has been that at this point the scene has begin already to sparkle with life. It may not be 'accurate' in relation to the play as as whole, but for the moment that is less important than making the words our own. Talk about it anyway with your partner, and share your ideas, excitement — and frustration if you have it.

Frustration, by the way, is not necessarily a sign that things are wrong. It is at about this point that some students will become concerned and even upset: "What does this have to do with the play? When are we going to read it? Am I close? I feel I'm working in the dark," and so on. I reply (infuriating them still more sometimes!) that this frustration is a wonderful sign of energy and commitment. At least it means they care, and making something out of nothing is always painful. It is what creative artists do, after all.

By not knowing too much of the characters at this point we have a real chance of 'grafting' them on to ourselves. Later there may have to be adjustments — but that first immediate, groping experience — of taking hold of a person through their words and phrases — never leaves us as we go more deeply into the play.

TEXT & TOUCH   EXERCISE V.2

1. Keep in your full consciousness the scene you have been working on.

2. One of you now sits, and the other, standing behind, massages the neck and shoulders, the back of the head and the upper back of the sitting partner. As the one doing the massaging works, he or she (once again in character) keeps repeating the name of the partner's character: so Torvald will say 'Nora' over and over, and as he works he will be once again playing the scene — perhaps remembering enough of it to be able to move through the main changes in attitude towards Nora during the scene.

During the massage, the partner receiving the massage also sits in character, responding to the hands of the masseur/se as to the other character — but in silence.

The value of massaging in this way takes place on many levels. First, touch in and of itself can release physical and psychological inhibitions. Secondly, the partner massaged can be not only helped to relax those muscles which can so easily tighten under stress, but along the way can re-act to the physical sensation of the massage as to the 'loving' but also dominating partner. For the masseur/se, the massaging is both a gentle, loving act and also an act which involves pressure — even a violation of a sort. The inter-relation of these two kinds of contact is like a physical version of the emotional relationship between the partners: mind and body working together. And finally, neither can see the face of the other during the massage. Neither need to conceal the facial expression of true feelings.

3. Change places and repeat the exercise in reverse.

The important thing to remember is that whatever feelings of passionate love, indifference, irritation or aggression are aroused, massage is still massage. The hands must always be controlled and gentle, whatever they would LIKE to be doing. If there is a conflict, it may emerge somewhere, but not in the pressure of the hands — perhaps in the breathing, or in the arms, or the face and neck of the masseur/se.

4. When both partners have completed the exercise, pick up the text again, and after a minute or two of silence, re-read the scene.

5. Discuss the effect, if any, that the massage exercise may have had — on the scene, on the relationship between the two characters, and on your emotional state.

Rest.

1. Now separate from your partner, and each go to different parts of the room with your text and play the scene once more — but this time play it separately and silently. What you must do is to 'listen' for your partner's voice as you remember or imagine him/her speaking the lines — and then imagine yourself (in silence) replying to the line you hear. In this way try to re-create the scene you have just read over, remembering your partner's voice via your sense of remembered hearing — or in your 'inner ear' as it is sometimes called.

Do this several times, until you have really sharpened your 'inner' hearing to detect the tones of your partner.

2. Now re-join your partner, and read the scene again. Did you remember your partner accurately? Has he/she changed in any way? Did the change have an effect on how you responded?

3. Put down your texts, and using all the 'experiences' you have so far been through, play the scene again, trying to remember as much of the text as you can. When you forget a line don't look it up but paraphrase it. KEEP GOING to the end.

You will probably find that you have remembered a surprising amount of your lines — and the lines you have to make up are often clues to how well you are linking up with the character.

After this, look up the text and check where you lost it — then play the scene again, without text. After three or four concentrated efforts like this, you will probably have mastered the whole thing. This approach to learning has results which surprise students who think they cannot 'memorize.' And the reason is simply that the experience has already begun to grow out of the words, and that what is remembered is as much that sequence of experience as the words themselves.

1. Stand alongside your partner facing a blank wall, with texts in your hands, or (preferably) without texts. Imagine yourself as two artists painting a mural on the wall. The brush strokes are your lines. Each line has colour. As you say each sentence, imagine it as a colour that you are brushing on to the wall — finding a place for it, a shape, a thickness and texture. Some brush-strokes will be bold and unpremeditated; others will be more tentative or subtle. Try as you go to hold a memory of the brush-strokes, their colour and shape. And also imagine the brush strokes of your partner, so that by the end of the scene the wall is a mass of colour and line — IN YOUR MEMORY.

Take your time in this exercise. If you need to, wait for a moment, planning your brush-stroke, so that you can be very specific and THOUGHTFUL about what you are doing and where you are doing it.

2. When you have finished, survey your work — and then turn to your partner and compare notes. What sort of a painting has each of you created? What are the colours? How did the 'style' of the painting come out? Was it a representational picture or an abstract? Did you find it easier to imagine your own brush-strokes than those of your partner? Did the complete 'picture' represent the conflict between the two characters? Did it balance the conflict, or was it over-weighted on one side or the other? Did your pictures turn out in any way alike?

3. And now once again return to the text, but this time first spend some minutes setting the scene, with furniture and props as available. The work you have done on it up to now should make decisions very simple.

4. Play the scene. Be sure not to try and engineer a climax at the end — let the action be like a cut or fade out in a film.

Summary

There is so much more one could say — but what we have been doing seems to explain itself. As I warned you, I have not talked much about the 'use of the voice' in this sequence of exercises, because when you are working on a scene you must in a sense forget about anything apart from the situation you are playing — let it dictate the way you speak.

But of course our work on voice never stops. And now in our final chapter we return to the process by which the voice conveys its message, both within real life situations and for an audience in a theatre. Of all 'dangerous' things we have discussed in relation to speech, 'diction' is the most dangerous of all. Too much awareness of it can get you talking like a phonetician. But too little will result in an audience throwing tomatoes!

Still connecting with the sigh-of-relief centre, start to produce a sound...(p.117)

VI.
Diction

There is something in the use of the voice which mechanical techniques cannot reach, and which self-conscious approaches seem to miss — that above everything else, the actor must experience what it feels like to BE his/her voice — to link the image created by the voice with the person activating the voice, the 'voicer'. If he/she can do this then the use and development of the voice should be straightforward. This is the central theme behind everything we have been doing so far together.

It sounds easy, the idea of BEING your voice, but if you think about YOUR relationship with YOUR voice, is it such a happy marriage? Is it YOU? Think about its stops and starts, its husky tones sometimes, its hard edge, its pleading, its occasional whine, its heavy barking stresses. Do you EXPLOIT these things — or do they happen naturally, simply reflecting your thoughts and feelings in a neutral way? Have any baby habits stayed with you in your voice — little tricks which were effective when you were a child and which you still fall back on when you want to get your way? Does your voice reflect truth — or, rather, what you would like people to believe? This question of naturalness versus artificiality is at the centre of the whole question of diction, and is the reason why I have called the study of diction 'dangerous'.

The difficulty is this: when you hear someone speak, you (normally) want to listen to what they are saying — in other words you want to understand what they mean by what they say. The speaker, similarly, wants you to understand. Speech employs words which mean something in themselves, and which combine with other words in such a way that the combination means other things. But speech is not simply a matter of words, and 'meaning' is not simply a matter of verbal formulas. Part of a speaker's meaning is contained in his/her feelings about what is being said and in the need to get the point across. Indeed, most theories of how language began suggest that it started with pre-verbal sounds that expressed physical wants and needs, and that these wants and needs still underlie even the driest speech.

Now everything that happens over and above the words in the act of speech can be thought of as 'diction': everything which the speaker does with the voice to convey what is meant to the people for whom it is spoken. At the beginning of our chapter on Articulation I described it as follows:

"Good diction means clarity of utterance, including not only the clear articulation of words but the effective interpretation of text, the control of tone, resonance and phrasing, of colour and pitch and volume, of rhythm and stress, and also the ability to project speech to all corners of the theatre."

Just as we can analyse the meaning of words and phrases and sentences, so we can also analyse the way that techniques of diction can help convey the speaker's meaning. In other words, we can actually study how to control what we say, how to utter it so that it affects and moves our listeners in the way that we intend. In classical times — and again in the Renaissance — this whole art of speaking was studied under the name of 'Rhetoric'.

Rhetoric was in fact the art of argument and of persuasion — skills required by public men such as lawyers, diplomats, politicians, philosophers and statesmen. And since the ability to persuade people was (and is) very much dependent on them believing in the speaker's sincerity, it followed that the student learned techniques for appearing to be sincere. And here we are again with that same paradox: the problem of how to 'appear to be' sincere without being insincere.

Here is an example. When the great Canadian hockey player Wayne Gretzky was at a press conference in August 1988 in order to announce that he had been traded from Edmonton (Canada) to Los Angeles, he stopped speaking, overcome with tears, and after two minutes of silence and some work with a handkerchief he gave up and someone else took over. Next day his ex-manager gave the impression that he thought Wayne had been 'acting' the tears — that it was a performance for the benefit of the public. True or false? Only Wayne could say for sure. But the fact is that the difference between someone pretending to be overcome, and someone who really is overcome, is non-existent if the 'acting' is good enough.

When you show your feelings, people usually believe you — but it is possible to LOOK AS THOUGH you are showing your feelings, and if it is done well enough people will still believe you. This is why studies on rhetoric were used in Shakespeare's time and earlier as actors' manuals. An actor's job is to get us to believe — or at least to 'suspend our disbelief' — that he/she really IS the character being played, and this means he/she must have the skill to appear to feel and experience what the character feels.

The things I have described as coming under the heading of diction — "the effective interpretation of text, the control of tone, resonance and phrasing, of colour and pitch and volume, of rhythm and stress; and also the ability to project speech to all corners of the theatre" — are all skills that can be learned. But the test of how well they are practised is whether the listener responds to them as separate things — "what a nice piece of phrasing!"..."what beautiful resonance!"..."What a clever handling of pitch and volume at that moment!"..."how wonderful, I am hearing every word!" — or whether the audience is entirely wrapped up in the meaning and the experience of what is being 'lived' through the speaking. "The art which conceals art," the Romans used to call it.

And herein lies the danger: if we mumble we may look real and feel totally sincere but people cannot hear what we are saying, but if we boom and over-articulate, we seem more interested in articulation than in meaning, and we lose the audience that way. If what we say lacks variety of tone colour, emphasis and rhythm, the ears of the audience do not have enough help to take in what is being said — but if the phrasing and colour and rhythm give the slightest sense of being artificially applied, then it all lifts off from the meaning and simply gives the impression that the actor loves the sound of his/her own voice. It is, like so many things, a matter of balance and judgement — based ultimately on the evidence of the actor's 'ear' and his/her intuition, sensitivity and intelligence. The accomplished actor, like anyone else with well-developed observation of human behaviour, will be able to hear the sound of untruth in his/her own voice, as much as in other people's, and adjust accordingly. Good diction comes in part from an alliance between the voice and the ear.

To understand how to approach diction, then, we must be able to see the difference between the POTENTIAL of the voice, and the actual USE of the voice.

The Potential of the Voice

The Potential of the voice is its capacity to operate within a number of spectrums of possibility. These can be very simply stated:

• The actor's voice must be capable of a wide spectrum of pitch, from high to low, and be able to shift rapidly from pitch to pitch as required, both in the inflection of words and in the 'melody' of sentences.

• The actor's voice must be capable of a wide spectrum of loudness, from loud to soft, and be able to shift quickly from one to the other. It must also be capable of being heard in all situations, even when the situation is intimate — there is a difference between quiet tone, and intimate but projected tone.

• The actor's voice must be capable of a wide spectrum of qualities, tone colour, timbre and accent: guttural, nasal, mellow, husky, hollow, shrill etc.

• The actor's voice must be capable of a wide spectrum in rate of delivery, and must be flexible in its capacity to change rate according to the needs of the situation.

All these represent the POTENTIAL of the actor's INSTRUMENT — in just the same way that a musical instrument has its potential and limitations.

The Use of the Voice

The actor whose voice possesses all the potential versatility and flexibility as described above must still be able to make judgements about what elements of his/her voice to use: what stresses, what melody of phrase, what rate(s) of delivery, what tone seems 'right' for every situation. And it is the ear — and also the whole mind's and body's 'feeling' — that must make the decision, based on the needs of the text, the relationship, the character and the situation.

It follows that the practice of good diction must take two paths, one of which opens up the actor to the furthest extent of the voice's potential; and the other which alerts the ear — and the body and mind — to the area of choice and judgement.

The Use of the voice corresponds to the way an instrumentalist uses his/her instrument to produce music — and it is here that work on voice meets work in the rehearsal room, and the speech teacher must give way to the director.

But the actor differs from the musician in that he/she is both instrument AND instrumentalist. Because of this, the separation of technical training of the voice from the use of it in actual stagework leads us into all the same dangers that my approach works to avoid. Everything that we have said, and everything we have done with colour and image-making in our exercises, is designed to reinforce the idea that technique is not a mechanical thing but DEVELOPS OUT OF THE NEED TO COMMUNICATE — and that it is not only our voice, but our body AND OUR WHOLE BEING that has this need. The following exercises should perhaps be called 'games' — they are fun to work with, and the spirit of them will help us in everything we do on the stage.

So To Speak

Vocal Explorations

Preparation:

Begin with the breathing exercises in Chapter II, finishing with our key sound: 'ha-ha-mmmmmm-mah'. Then repeat exercise III.3 (p.54) — the one that exercises our facial muscles. These are essential preliminaries. They are crucial to all our vocal exploration, and must become part of your regular work, supplemented by your own selection of the other exercises we have been working with. Let all of them become second nature to you, like the steps of a dance.

EXPLORING RANGE	EXERCISE VI.1

1. Stand in alignment, making sure that you are free of tension, and read the following text. It should be written out large enough for it to be read from a distance, so that you do not have to hold anything in your hand.

"There is a tide in the affairs of men,
Which, taken at the flood, leads on to fortune."
(Shakespeare: *Julius Caesar* Act 4 Sc. 3)

2. Now leave the text for the moment and give a long, enjoyable sigh of relief. Do this several times, always being aware of where the sigh of relief is coming from: the centre of your body. As we learned to do before, find a pleasurable reason for the sigh, so that it is connected with your feelings.

3. Still connecting with the sigh-of-relief centre start to produce a sound, imagining that it comes from the tail-bone and travels slowly up the spine. It begins in a very low register and as it travels it rises slowly higher and higher, until it is resonating in your head. Use the sound 'ee'. When you reach the top, take a breath and (from the sigh-

of-relief impulse) begin on a note as high or, if possible, higher than the one you ended on and let it travel back down your spine as it returns to the low register. Take the sound up and down on these return journeys several times, until you feel you have established an open channel for the sound, and can bring it out at its top level with no strain or tension. You may find yourself raising the jaw for the high note, or even standing on tip-toe — and even pushing your jaw into the larynx when you start at the bottom. Become aware of this and don't let those muscles push you around.

(Singers are often told, in fact, to reverse these tendencies — to picture the head tilting down a little for the high range, and raising up a little for the low notes. This is the right idea, but I have found it is important that this is no more than a 'picture' or sensation. If the head actually makes a definite muscular action of tilting up and down, the air passage or channel for sound can be constricted. Besides it can look as silly as its opposite, and has nothing to do with communication.)

4. Now add different consonants in front of the sound, and repeat the exercise three or four times with each consonant: 'kee,' 'lee,' 'mee,' 'se,' 'tee.' Never lose touch with the impulse of the sigh-of-relief that we started with: it is this which keeps your throat muscles easy and relaxed, and also keeps your emotions involved through the 'relief' of the pleasureful sigh. Practice will show how vitally important this is.

5. Now let us get this further inside our 'body's psychology' (as Michael Chekhov calls it.)[32] Returning to the 'kee' sound, start once again low (with the sigh-of-relief impulse) but this time, as you make the sound, start dropping the neck forward and then continue dropping the head forward and down, rolling the spine slowly downward until your head hangs between your knees. When you are fully down, connect once again with the sigh-of-relief impulse, and then, as before, reach for a higher note than the one you finished on (with no strain, of course) and start coming up again to the upright position. The sound and the movement should come from the same impulse and

stop and start more or less at the same time.

If you become dizzy, don't panic — take a moment to rest, and then continue.

Do this several times, and rest.

6. Now take the text with which we began, and standing in alignment once more, speak the two lines in place of the 'kee' sound — the first line ascending, and the second line descending. Don't at this point try and make sense of the words — just use them to shape the sound:

```
               which
        men    taken
        of       at
        affairs    the
          the        flood
          in          leads
          tide          on
          a              to
          is              fortune.
        There
```

(Start)   **(Finish)**

Never lose the sense of the sigh-of-relief impulse, which makes each utterance your own. Remember, the sigh is a feeling — your own particular feeling.

Always work to extend your voice at either end of its range. Regular practice of this exercise, eight to twelve minutes a day, will rapidly extend your comfortable vocal range, providing a greater spectrum of possibilities for the expression of feelings.

Many books will print exercises in inflection with arrows going up to show us a rising inflection and down to show a falling inflection, etc. Once again I say that we do have to think about these things, but that any attempt to imitate arrows is going to run into the danger of being mechanical. Let us work another way...

1. We will be uttering the sound 'oh!' in such a way that it will suggest the meanings listed below. Start with the first (slight surprise) and then let your partner imitate you. Then let your partner initiate the second (great surprise) and imitate him/her in your turn. Continue down the list.

> Slight surprise
> Great surprise
> Polite interest
> Doubt
> Marked indifference
> Disbelief
> Disappointment
> Pity
> Disgust
> Sarcasm
> Happy surprise
> Horror
> Fear

Remember, this should not be treated as an exercise to create 'instant' acted emotional states, but as a test of your ear-voice collaboration. Exaggerate the emphasis and tone of your voice as much as you can, so that each exclamation is as different as possible from the others. The exercise is designed to give you a sense of the wide range of meanings that can be conveyed simply by the different inflections of one syllable, and once again to extend your tonal range. 'Feeling' each of the meanings is not of course forbidden, but there is a real danger of 'hamming' this swift sequence of displayed emotions. Sincere emotions don't often get switched on and off so rapidly. Think of it then as simply a voice 'range' exercise.

2. Now exchange 'Oh!'s with your partner, this time randomly finding your own inflections.

3. Now here is an exchange from the scene we worked with in the last chapter, from the final scene in Ibsen's *A Doll's House*:

    "You have never loved me."   *"— What do you mean?"*

Speak the exchange several times with your partner, each of you experimenting with different meanings. Then start having fun with it — exaggerate — go crazy. Repeat a word or phrase whenever you feel like it. Let your face join in the fun — make faces. Now let your whole body join in, so that the whole of you is alive, weaving and swooping, twisting, stretching and bending. Allow yourself to become more and more excited, and finally to reach a high point of activity and sound — only being careful not to force or strain the vocal cords by tensing them and then pushing air through them.

4. Take a short text of your own choice (preferably something you have already learned) or pick out other exchanges from the same text, like:
    "What is this cold, set face?"   *"Sit down."*

    or *"I shall not sleep tonight."*   *"But my dear.."*

Give your voice full — wild — free range to swoop and slide up and down its range while speaking the lines.

Round it off — and rest.

You will find that this exaggerating of inflection and tone gives you a chance to explore your range in an adventurous way — it lets us break out of our usual carefully controlled, buttoned-up manner, and be mad for a while. Notice, by the way, that being cheerfully mad means letting go, which is another form of relaxation. Afterwards, if you perform the text 'naturally,' you will feel the difference: those newly awakened parts of your range are now available to express your feelings.

Loudness & Softness

There are voice teachers who wince when the word 'loudness' is mentioned; and surely nothing is worse than hearing someone being told to 'speak louder,' because of the danger of forcing and therefore of phoniness. But on the other hand, as anyone who has been in a theatre audience will agree, there is nothing more upsetting than not being able to hear. And when you are not hearing, the reason is simple. The actor, whether speaking too quietly or too unclearly, is not speaking in a way that can be heard. There is the famous story of Tyrone Guthrie in New York who, when working with a group of deeply sincere method actors, finally interrupted a dress rehearsal from the end of the auditorium, with a booming voice and in a splendid upper-class British accent, "SORRY CHAPS: CAN'T HEAR THE FUCKING WORDS!" There are moments when delicate handling of the psychological problem of inaudibility has to give way to plain facts.

So To Speak

1. Stand in alignment, and count from one to ten, taking a breath before each number.

Listen to the sound and imagine it carrying — every particle of each word — to every part of the room where you are working. People talk of a 'carrying' voice. Can you think what that means? Say the numbers in a non-carrying voice, and then again return to the job of letting the whole room hear. Notice how the carrying power is generated by breath — how you tend to stretch out the vowels when you WANT the voice to carry. It is through the breath that the vowels transmit the carrying power — and the difference between the sounds of the different vowels becomes very important to the clarity of what we say. Notice, also, that the need for clarity will tend to slow down the rhythm of what you are saying. All the time, LISTEN! Only you are going to be able to gauge how much sound is needed to communicate in any situation — you are your own monitor.

2. Now speak the names of ten countries in succession, concentrating in the same way on the 'carrying' of the voice. Never yell, and never strain your vocal cords. If you hear your voice starting to crack, you have started to lose control of it, and can do damage. Breath is the energy source, not muscle tension.

3. Cup your hands in front of your mouth, and repeat into your hands the names of the countries. Then take your hands away and repeat the names. Notice the difference.

4. Take the following text, and read it imagining the following different situations:

> i. A conversation with a small group of people in a room.

> ii. A talk to a room crowded with people standing and sitting everywhere — some perhaps even in the doorway and stretching out to the corridor.

> iii. A public address to a large group of people in a theatre, auditorium or assembly hall — without a public address system.

Here is the text:

> "*Every man's house will be fair and decent, soothing to his mind and helpful to his work: all the works of man that we live amongst and handle will be in harmony with nature, will be reasonable and beautiful: yet all will be simple and inspiriting, not childish, nor enervating; for as nothing of beauty and splendour that man's mind and hand may compass shall be wanting from our public buildings, so in no private dwelling will there be any signs of waste, pomp, or insolence, and every man shall have his share of the best.*"
>
> "*It is a dream, you may say, of what has never been and never will be; true, it has never been, and therefore my hope is the greater that it one day will be: true, it is a dream; but dreams have before now come about of things so good and necessary to us. And I am here tonight to ask you to help in realizing this dream...this hope.*"[33]

Notice what effects the different situations have on the way you speak. Can you move easily from one to the other? Can you IMAGINE the voice needed for each situation, and make the adjustment? These adjustments are essential for the actor.

Exploring Distance	Exercise VI.4

Finally let us try one 'distance' game which I learned as a young student at the Conservatory.

1. Face your partner, but about twenty feet away from one another, and start a conversation. Continue for a few minutes. What did the distance do to your conversation? Did the gap between you make the talk less personal? This is sometimes described as a 'public' distance.

2. Now halve the distance between you and your partner and continue talking for another couple of minutes. See if you notice any change in the quality of your talk. This has been called a 'social' distance.

3. Close the gap between you and your partner to no more than three feet, and continue talking at this 'personal' distance. Discuss the change caused by closing the gap.

4. Now be face to face, and almost nose to nose, and keep talking. How does it feel now?

All these different situations affect the way we talk and the way we communicate — and even the things we talk about: the medium is the message. By moving through these various exercises, we come to realize how much our voice adjusts (often unconsciously) to varying problems and space relationships. It is not a mechanical process, but one that involves our relationship with other people, and the assessment we have to make of how we are to place our contact with them. We should also be aware that loudness doesn't necessarily mean audibility — the volume of sound must work hand in hand with articulation.

Note: I have said several times "listen to your voice," "monitor your voice." This is essential when you are training your ear. But you must be careful that with this kind of listening you do not become your own audience. You are listening ON BEHALF of the audience — putting yourself into their ears. People who cannot be heard when they speak are people who cannot imagine what it is like to be listening. People who are sensitive to the sound of their own voice will immediately be aware of an acoustical problem and will almost automatically adjust their delivery to take account of it. But the reason is always the same — YOU WISH TO COMMUNICATE HONESTLY AND FREELY!

So To Speak

Rate of Delivery

The actor's voice must have enough agility to be able to utter words rapidly without being incomprehensible, and enough sustaining power and intensity to utter them slowly without being boring. Exercises designed to work the muscles of the tongue, lips and face have already been dealt with under the heading of articulation, and no rapid delivery is possible without well-developed and well-controlled muscles in these areas.

But there is more to rapid delivery than good articulatory muscles. The pace of speech delivery is in general a product of the speed at which the actor (or the character being played) is thinking. A deliberate thinker is likely to speak deliberately, and if the ideas are not complex the audience may easily lose interest — their thoughts run ahead of the speech. There is a tendency for anxious directors to tell a ponderous actor to 'speak faster.' But the problem lies in the speed of thought — the direction should be to 'think faster.'

It might be imagined that the speed at which we think is part of our personality and is unchangeable. We all know people who seem to have a quicksilver response to everything around them. They move fast and talk fast because their minds process and produce information and reactions at high speed. These people are often fun to be with, because we have to stay alert to keep up with them, and this is exciting. The quicksilver actor has the same effect on an audience provided that they can keep up with him/her. But there are situations in which this kind of quicksilver mentality can also be tiresome, because there are times when we need deliberate thought, and a chance to weigh situations slowly — or a chance to adjust emotionally to a shock of some kind. Similarly, in the theatre, there are times for ceremony, when the characters in the play must be able to take in momentous news or unexpected changes of situation. The 'deposition' scene in *Richard II* (Act IV, sc. 1) shows Richard giving up his crown under pressure from Bolingbroke. A rapid scene would make the whole thing ridiculous. But even here ponderousness must be avoided: we must sense the intensity of feeling both of Richard and of the onlookers.

This capacity to adjust pace to situation is not strictly a vocal skill — it is part of the skill of acting. But I have listed it here simply as one of the 'potentials' of the voice, and here are some exercises which at least draw the actor's attention to the rate of thought and of delivery.

1. Take a few minutes with your partner to learn the following passage from the poem *Tarantella* by Hilaire Belloc:

> *Do you remember an Inn, Miranda?*
> *Do you remember an Inn?*
> *And the tedding and the spreading*
> *Of the straw for a bedding,*
> *And the fleas that tease in the High Pyrenees,*
> *And the wine that tasted of the tar,*
> *And the cheers and the jeers of the young muleteers*
> *(Under the vine of the dark verandah)?*
> *Do you remember an Inn, Miranda,*
> *Do you remember an Inn?*[34]

Now take a medium-sized ball and face your partner at a distance of some twelve feet. You start first. Throw the ball to your partner, and as the ball leaves your hand start speaking the text. Your partner silently catches the ball and throws it back, and all the time you continue speaking until the ball returns to your hands. See how far you can get with the text: speak as rapidly as possible, but the words must be clear and intelligible — let your partner tell you how well you do.

Do the exercise three times, until you have found what seems to be your fastest intelligible rate of delivery. Then it is your partner's turn to do the same thing, with you silently catching the ball and throwing it back. See who can regularly get further in the text.

2. Now each take a step closer, and start again, this time with a reduced distance between you. Try to reach your previous stopping point in the text — but still without losing intelligibility.

3. Repeat the exercise, getting closer each time. If you wish, you can extend your time by throwing the ball higher in the air. Even so, your time will slowly contract, and your articulatory muscles will have to work harder and harder. Stop when you like. Rest.

By the way, this can also be used as a dialogue exercise. Speak the first line as you throw the ball, and your partner speaks the second line as he/she returns it. There are many variations, which you can think up on your own.

4. Now sit in a chair, with your partner standing beside you. When you are both ready, your partner leaves your side and starts walking towards the door. You know that going through the door means catastrophe for you both. Try and persuade him/her as rapidly as you can and in your own words not to go through the door. It is up to your partner — and to your own persuasiveness — whether he/she stops, slows down or turns, or continues moving. In the end, though, he/she will go through the door, signifying the end of the exercise.

Reverse roles.

5. Now pick up an object and sell it to your partner as though you are in a market and he/she is a passing customer. Like any such salesperson you have only a few seconds to attract and hold your audience.

Reverse roles.

Finally, both pick up an object and sell them simultaneously to one another.

6. Now, each in turn, recite the passage from *Tarantella* at the speed which you gauge is appropriate for the poem.

Discuss the effects of the different exercises.

Voice Quality

An actor's voice, which needs to sound at different times like the voices of the many different people whose characters are portrayed on stage, must clearly be capable of different qualities, different kinds of sound, different personalities.

As a corollary of this, the voice must be capable of being more or less 'neutral' — free of specific vocal characteristics. It may be very effective for an actor to adopt a lisp for a certain role: but if an actor has a lisp whenever he/she speaks, then this will clearly limit the versatility of the voice. There is a similar problem if the actor is unable to pronounce clearly the difference between an 'r' and a 'w', or if his/her voice is unable to free itself of nasality, breathiness, throaty sound, whistling 's', stammer, stutter, shrillness or stridency.

Voices which have one or more of these characteristics as a result of a structural handicap or physical oddity of some kind (gaps in the teeth, misshapen teeth or protruding jaw, high or cleft palate, stringed tongue etc.) are in need of professional and perhaps surgical treatment, and cannot be dealt with here. But it is my experience that when vocal oddities have come about merely as a result of psychological laziness or stress, they will right themselves by diligent application to the vocal work described in these pages. The worst response to a sibilant 's' or a 'rabbity r', I have found, is to draw the actor's attention to it too much. The freeing process whch we have been working with liberates the voice from these problems without any special treatment or therapy. "I am not going to tell you what is wrong with the speech sounds you make," I often say, "it is just that the sounds are not yet your own." If you zero in on a new student and tell him/her about their defects, the inhibitions (which in fact may have caused the problems in the first place) tend to get worse.

I do find it important, though, to be honest and direct in advising students when they clearly do have structural problems. Two students of mine have had serious defects: one with a 'lantern' jaw, the other with protruding teeth, and both conditions causing vocal distortions as well as problems with physical appearance. Both had surgery, and both are now highly successful artists — one of them the star of a television series.

Let us concentrate, then, on the development of voice quality.

The actor who is capable of neutral speech — speech without impediments or oddities — still needs to be aware of what the voice must do to become the voice of another person. Once again, as with all questions of diction, the dangers are considerable. When people like Rich Little 'impersonate' famous personalities, they copy mannerisms both of speech and movements: a turn or shake of the head, a turn of phrase or a characteristic tone, puts us in mind of the original in the same way that a political cartoon strikes us. No good actor wants to be considered an impersonator or mimic: when Olivier spent six months lowering his vocal range in order to play the part of Othello in the style of a West African leader such as Nkrumah, the critic Kenneth Tynan described the result as the finest piece of bad acting he had ever seen. And yet we have to recognize that the way people talk often reveals something of their character. The ability to 'find' the voices of characters in a way which is not superficial but which reveals some essence of personality takes years of observation and experience.

Here is one exercise which can get you started on the journey:

EXPLORING VOICE QUALITY   EXERCISE VI.6

1. Face your partner and each study the other for three minutes, in silence. Be relaxed, but not rigid. Move around a little, drink a cup of coffee, shift on your chair, look occasionally away. And during this time, watch each other and try to determine in your mind what it is that characterises the look and behaviour of your partner. Why would you recognize him/her in silhouette? Try and pick three characteristics.

2. Now each of you in turn tell a story to the other, lasting two or three minutes. The listener should hear the story, but also must try once again to detect what it is in the voice that characterises the speaker. Close the eyes some of the time as you listen. These are some of the areas to be observed:

Is the voice harsh or soft? Nasal or throaty? Is the tone mellow and rounded, or reedy and thin? Where is the average pitch of the voice?

What sort of range does it operate in — high? Low? Medium? Does it work within just a few notes close together, or wide swings from high to low? How strongly does the voice stress words? Is there a characteristic inflection or melody; and if there is, does it suggest a mood of any kind — complaining, ironic, sentimental, anxious to please? Are there interruptions of any kind — throat-clearing, or hesitations, or repeated corrections, or frequent uses of a word or phrase?

3. Discuss with each other what you have noticed. In trying to explain what you heard in the voice, try and imitate vocal characteristics, but only as part of a serious demonstration of what you heard: do not try to create a caricature or impersonation.

4. Now each tell the other's story, trying to 'be' the other person. This may end up in laughter, but don't let this obscure what you have learned: that there is a lot to be gained from close attention to the way people talk, and that the ear is an essential guide.

This is a habit of observation that can continue every day of your life — any time you hear someone speak, in the café, pub or waiting room, or on radio or television. Develop a habit of listening to 'kinds' of voices, and to linking the character of people to the way they speak. If you can, watch them at the same time, and see how the connection functions between bodily movement and vocal expression.

The Use Of The Voice

Another set of exercises? No, not this time! In fact, this is where I tiptoe out of the room and leave you to continue our work on your own.

Why? Because all speech teachers must draw a line where voice training ends and THE USE OF THE VOICE BEGINS. For the purpose of this book, I have drawn the line right here: the point where the voice must start to work directly with questions of interpretation and character — the point, in fact, where the director takes over from the voice teacher, or where real life takes over from exercise.

Not so long ago I was at a conference, where a distinguished acting teacher was giving an account of his methods to an international group of professional directors, actors and teachers. After he finished an old Russian director got up and said cuttingly, "Exercises! Exercises! Exercises!" Perhaps he was being unfair, but the point was well made. In the end, our exercises must give way to the thing itself: the use of the voice in actual performance in front of an audience.

Your vocal work as an actor must now draw its motivations and its energy from the needs of each text and the demands of each production. And your vocal work as a person must test itself in the play of daily life, with all its challenges.

But wherever you are, and whatever you are doing, treasure that voice of yours! And don't forget: the work we have shared on this journey together will always be here, and always available to help you meet those challenges.

Bon Voyage!

A Final Word

This book attempts to detail a process of voice development which, as I have already mentioned, has been described as 'impossible to write down'. Perhaps these efforts only prove the correctness of the statement! Certainly, as I work through the various headings of each chapter, each section, each exercise, I again and again become irritated by the need to break up the material into separate areas. These neat compartments suggest that things can be dealt with in an orderly way, one at a time.

In fact, the process I explore here and which I have been engaged in for many years, is an entirely 'holistic' one. Every exercise contains within it elements of all other exercises. We move from one element to another, not in a linear way, but as the spirit and mood of the moment suggests. Slowly, as our work together accumulates, we find we do everything that has to be done.

This sense of interconnectedness has always affected my work as a teacher in the classroom. The prepared lesson is always there, but intuition and the sense of occasion may well tell me that NOW is the moment to move in an unexpected direction with a particular student or class. Perhaps it is the sun suddenly pouring in through a high window and lifting our mood, or a spark of emotional intensity which has to be allowed to catch fire, or a 'breakthrough' to be followed up. Perhaps there is some personal stress to deal with, or a chance event which makes us laugh and alters the flow of things.

This ability to improvize, to respond spontaneously and with confidence, is something for which my experience in Ottawa helped prepare me. In any case, it is part of the very essence of the theatre. No lesson that follows a rigid, inflexible plan is going to catch the amazing multiplicity that we need to be able to cope with in our craft and also in our lives.

This book, then, is not the summing up of a 'method'. It is simply a storehouse of ideas and experiences which have been of value to many people over the years.

Please use it and enjoy it.

Footnotes

Introduction
1. McLuhan, Marshall *The Medium is the Message*, New York: Bantam 1967, p. 18.
2. Mentioned in Bronowski, J. *The Identity of Man*, New York: Natural History Press 1971, p. 126.
3. Mead, Margaret *Male and Female*, London: Gollancz 1949, p. 55.
4. Higham, Charles *Charles Laughton: An Intimate Biography*, New York: Doubleday 1976, p. 7.
5. Higham, ibid. p. 8.

Before We Begin

6. Linklater, Kristin *Freeing the Natural Voice*, New York: Drama Book Specialists 1976, p. 2.
7. Samuels, Mike and Nancy *Seeing with the Mind's Eye*, New York: Random House 1975, p. xi.

Chapter 1: Posture

8. Statistics quoted in Barlow, Wilfred *The Alexander Technique*, New York: Knopf 1981, p. 12.
9. Miller, Jonathan *The Body In Question*, London: MacMillan 1982, p.308.
10. Bernhardt, Colin: unpublished manuscript.

Chapter 2: Breath

11. Wordsworth, William *The Prelude*, Bk. 1, l.401.
12. Leonard, George *The Silent Pulse*, New York: Dutton 1978, p. xii.

Chapter 3: Relaxation

13. Beary, J. and Benson, H. "A Simple Psycho-physiologic Technique which Elicits the Hypometabolic Changes of the Relaxation

Response." Quoted in Alexander, F. *Psychosomatic Medicine.*" New York: Norton 1950, p. 36.

14. Stanislavsky, Constantin *An Actor Prepares,* New York: Theatre Arts Books 1982, p. 94.

15. Plato *The Republic,* translated by Francis Cornford, New York: OUP 1945, p.93.

16. Stanislavsky, ibid. p. 95.

17. Quoted in Doe Lang's *The Charisma Book,* New York: Wyden Books 1980 p. 44.

18. The alphabet of Sanscrit has fifty letters, and it is the only known language that includes all the sounds that infants make as they are learning to speak. The sounds associated with mantras come from Sanscrit: this has been cited as one of the reasons for the effect of mantra sounds on the human organism.

19. See footnote 5.

20. Stanislavsky, ibid. p. 67.

21. Bates, William *Better Eyesight Without Glasses,* New York: Henry Holt 1918. Quoted in Samuels, Mike and Nancy, ibid. p. 234.

Chapter 4: Articulation

22. Steiner, Rudolf *Eurythmy as Visible Speech,* London: Rudolf Steiner Press 1984, p. 12.

23. Chekhov, Michael *Lessons for the Professional Actor,* New York: PAJP 1985, pp. 25-6.

24. Anderson, Virgil A. *Training the Speaking Voice,* New York: OUP 1977, p. 293.

25. Virgil Anderson's book (see above) covers the field very thoroughly: see pp. 355-412.

26. Steiner, Rudolf, ibid. pp. 29-31.

27. Stanislavsky, Constantin *Building A Character,* New York: Theatre Arts Books 1949, p. 84.

Chapter 5: Text

28. Hamlet's speech to the players, Act III scene 2.

29. We think of the technique of improvizing scenes as a modern one but the great Sarah Bernhardt apparently practised it a hundred years ago. A critic sat in on a rehearsal in 1887 and wrote: "It is quite a scene; she scorns the script and plays from memory, sometimes finding words more precise, clearer...often she discovers in this way a particularly felicitous gesture, sprung from her own experience, or a particularly admirable phrasing." Quoted in Salmon, E. (ed.), *Bernhardt and the Theatre of her Time*, London: Greenwood Press 1984, p. 42.

30. The concept of microcosm/macrocosm comes from the Cabbala and was brought widely into Western use by the 'Hermetic' philosophers of the sixteenth century. For a general explanation of the ideas of microcosm/macrocosm see Frances A. Yates's *The Art of Memory*, London: Routledge and Kegan Paul 1966, p. 160. For more on the 'humours' see Ralph Metzner's *Know Your Type* New York: Doubleday 1979, pp. 37-54.

31. Sprat, Thomas *History of the Royal Society*, 1667.

Chapter 6: Diction

32. Chekhov, Michael *To the Actor*, New York: PAJP 1953, pp. 1-20.
33. Morris, William *My Hopes and Fears for Art*, London: Longman 1898, pp. 36-7.

Bibliography

Some of the books in this list have already been referred to in the foot-notes, and are detailed here again for ease of reference. The other books listed have influenced my work and ideas in a more general way. I have grouped them under separate headings, although naturally there are overlaps in their subject matter.

SPEECH SKILLS

Anderson, Virgil A. *Training The Speaking Voice*, New York: Oxford University Press 1977.

Berry, Cicely *Voice And The Actor*, London: Harrap 1973.

Curry, S.S. *Mind And Voice*, Boston: Expression Co. 1910.

Linklater, Kristin *Freeing The Natural Voice*, New York: Drama Book Specialists 1976.

Machlin, Evangeline *Speech For The Stage*, New York: Theatre Arts Books 1966.

Steiner, Rudolf *Creative Speech*, New York: Anthroposophic Press 1985.

Steiner, Rudolf *Speech And Drama*, London: Rudolf Steiner Press 1986.

Turner, Clifford J. *Voice And Speech In The Theatre*, New York: Pitman Publishers 1975.

Werbeck-Svardstrom V. *Uncovering Of The Voice*, London: Rudolf Steiner Press 1975.

ACTING AND ACTING SKILLS

Benedetti, Robert L. *The Director At Work*, New Jersey: Prentice Hall 1985.

Black, Lendley C. *Mikhail Chekov As Actor, Director And Teacher*, Michigan: U.M.I. Research Press 1987.

Bowskill, Derek *Drama And The Teacher*, London: Pitman 1974.

Chekhov, Michael *To The Actor*, New York: Harper & Row 1953. "Lessons For The Professional Actor". New York: *Performing Arts Journal* 1985.

Grotowski, Jerzy *Towards A Poor Theatre*, New York: Simon & Shuster 1968.

140   *So To Speak*

Johnstone, Keith *Improv,* London/Boston: Faber 1979.

Moore, Sonia *The Stanislavski System,* New York: Viking Press 1965.

Scheckner, Richard *Environmental Theatre,* New York: Hawthorn Books 1973.

Slade, Peter *Child Drama,* London: University of London Press 1954.

Spolin, Viola *Improvisation For The Theatre* Chicago: N.W. University Press 1963.

Stanislavsky, C. *An Actor Prepares,* New York: Theatre Art Books 1936.

Stanislavsky, C. *Building A Character,* New York: Theatre Art Books 1949.

Stanislavsky, C. *Creating A Role* New York: Theatre Art Books 1961.

Way, Brian *Development Through Drama,* London: Longman 1987.

GENERAL BOOKS

Herrigel, Eugen *Zen And The Art Of Archery,* New York: Vintage Books 1971.

Houston, Jean *Listening To The Body,* New York: Delta 1978.

Jones, Alex *Seven Mansions Of Color,* California: DeVorss 1982.

Jung, Carl G. *Man And His Symbols,* New York: Doubleday 1969.

Leonard, George *The Silent Pulse,* New York: Bantam 1981.

Reyes, L.E. *Toning,* California: DeVorss 1982.

Actor, director and teacher, **Colin Bernhardt** has been an inspiring guide in the development of the natural voice for thousands of participants in classes and workshops in Canada and internationally. He has worked with Stratford Festival Shakespeareans, Metropolitan Opera singers, theatre and film artists as well as writers, teachers, and communicators in myriad disciplines. He is a theatre director, co-founder of the Atlantic Theatre Festival in Wolfville, Nova Scotia as well as Associate Professor of English at Acadia University and a member of the Writing faculty of the Banff Centre School of Fine Arts. *So to Speak* is his first book. Colin Bernhardt lives in Wolfville, Nova Scotia.